YEAR OF THE LORD'S FAVOUR

A Homiliary for the Roman Liturgy

VOLUME 1
The Sanctoral Cycle

Aidan Nichols, OP

GRACEWING

'The orthodox is, in the best and most humane sense, a rhetorician—he is adapting the material of the Christian Tradition, in order to persuade his audience either to conversion or repentance, a *metanoia*; yet the "form" is to be distinguished from "the Catholic doctrine", to which the particular rhetorical forms are obedient and implicitly refer.'

Stephen Thomas on Newman

'Preaching is the monstrance of the Gospel, offered to God, addressed to men, an act of worship whereby Christ is manifested to the world in terms both of the promises the Gospel offers and of the demands it places.'

Charles Journet

First published in England in 2012
by
Gracewing
2 Southern Avenue
Leominster
Herefordshire HR6 0QF
United Kingdom
www.gracewing.co.uk

ISBN 978 085244 791 8

Typeset by Gracewing

Cover design by Bernardita Peña Hurtado

CONTENTS

GENERAL INTRODUCTION

Preaching begins a long way away from us. And yet at the same time it starts off closer to us than we are to ourselves.

It takes its rise from the eternal generation of God the Word, the divine Logos, before time began. The Word is the everlasting Meaning of the Father. By that same Word we too were made. So what our lives 'mean' is ultimately what they mean in God and even (we can say) what God means in and by them.

When, two millennia past, the life of the Word entered our world and became incarnate, it took the form of the man Jesus, the humanity that the Word assumed. The mission of Jesus Christ *is* the eternal proceeding of the Word from the Father, now taking place in new conditions, in time and space, and so in history and geography, in language and culture. This gives the preaching of Jesus a unique quality, which no other human utterance has ever possessed. It is God's own interpretation of God, his interpretation of his life as it is in itself, and of his plan for us.

The preaching of the Church is not just speech about this unique preaching by Christ, the Word incarnate. It is also a continuation of that preaching. Jesus commissions the apostles as his legates, telling them, whoever hears you hears me, and promises them his Holy Spirit to remind them of everything he has said to them and to guide them into all truth.

This apostolic mission is confided to all Christians when they are initiated into the Church by Baptism and Confirmation, and it is given in a more solemn and representative way to deacons, priests and bishops by the sacrament of Holy Orders. In the Dominican Order, uniquely, that mission also exists in a third fashion, as a 'charism', a free gift of the Holy Spirit, to be lived out as the centre of an existence that is dedicated to God by a monastic form of life, structured by liturgical prayer and observance.

In preaching, our duty is to speak about the Word in the Church. This makes preaching a pre-eminently contemplative task. It also makes it an ecclesial one, in communion with the bishop who is the primary preacher of the local church in every place. The mediaeval preaching manuals go further. They insist that preaching is not only an evangelical office but also an angelical one the latter being the explanation of why, in Byzantine iconography, the preacher St John the Baptist is shown sprouting wings, and the same is true in the art of Latin Christendom for St Vincent Ferrer, the fourteenth century Dominican widely regarded as quite simply the most effective preacher in the history of the Western church.

The homilies presented here are in the Dominican tradition of doctrinal preaching: a preaching of Scripture which takes doctrine as guide to the clarification of the Bible's main lines. Without doctrine, we should find it more difficult to see the biblical wood for the profusion of the Scriptural trees. Doctrine is necessary to preachers because in its absence the Scriptural claims and themes do not hang together. They do not of their own accord organize themselves into a religion a person can live by: a coherent vision of truth, and a picture of human excellence that is imitable because it makes sense as a whole. Where doctrine is not permitted to serve this purpose, we can be sure that some other scheme of thought will be brought in to do the job instead. That is when theology becomes ideology, rather than a service to the Word of God in the message of the Church.

So the role of doctrine in preaching is to ensure that preaching maintains its full and proper scope. Though the inspiration of preaching has its genesis in the grace of God, more interior to us than we are to ourselves, that grace is never purely individual in character. The 'grace of the Word' always has a reference to *Ecclesia*, the Mystical Body which mediates all the grace that is given by Christ the Head. So, precisely as a fruit of grace, preaching is necessarily related to ecclesial consciousness. Doctrine ensures that preaching does not fall short of its true dimensions which are co-extensive with the biblical revelation, the faith of the Church. Preaching about the lives of the saints is a partial exception to these principles and yet every saint throws light on some aspect of the mystery of Christ and the Church.

This Homiliary provides suggestions for doctrinally-based preaching for the entire Church year. In turning these homilies into decent English prose, something of the immediacy of *viva voce* presentation is inevitably lost. And in any case they were delivered to relatively specialized congregations: either in University chaplaincies (in Edinburgh and Cambridge) or in University cities (Cambridge and Oxford). One size does not fit all. But they are intended, of course, not for reproduction in their entirety, but only to provide stimuli for preachers elsewhere. My hope is that they could be useful in this way.

The first volume deals with the Sanctoral Cycle: the celebrations of Christ, our Lady, and the saints to which are added a handful of homilies for commemorations of the faithful departed. For some of the greatest feast days two or more homilies have been provided. All the feasts and obligatory memorias celebrated in the Roman rite Church have been included as well as a light sprinkling of optional memorias where the writer feels a special devotion (notably concerning certain doctors of the Church). Among the saints additionally selected are a number which figure not in the General Calendar of the Latin church but in the calendars of the Order of Preachers and the Diocese of East Anglia respectively. As I have lived all my priestly life as a Dominican and over two-thirds of it in Cambridge, this was quasi-inevitable. I hope these saints and blesseds will be of some interest. They represent an important principle of preaching: it should not be so generally directed as to refuse the claims of a 'local habitation and a name'. By the same principle I have included specifically Dominican commemorations of the dead likewise.

This first volume of *Year of the Lord's Favour* ends with homilies for the Dedication of the Cathedral Church, for the Solemnities of the Lord in Ordinary Time (except for Christ the King), and, as a coda, for the Blessed Virgin Mary *de Sabbato* the commemoration of our Lady 'on Saturdays'.

The second, third, and fourth volumes of the Homiliary cover between them the Temporal Cycle of the Church of the Roman rite. The second volume furnishes texts for the Privileged Seasons: Advent, Christmastide, Lent and Eastertide; the third for Sundays through the Year, and the fourth for Weekdays through the Year. The biblical readings presupposed are those of the Roman Lectionary as revised by Pope Paul VI. For Sundays through the Year (with the exception of the Solemnity of Christ the King), a homily is provided for each year of the Lectionary's three-year Sunday cycle. For Weekdays through the Year, a homily based on the Gospel of the day can be used in both years of the corresponding two-year weekday cycle. A scattering of weekday homilies is also offered for use in either the first or the second year, so as to do greater justice to the Old Testament lections and the New Testament epistles.

Biblical citations are from either of the two versions licensed at different times for liturgical reading in England, the Revised Standard Version (Catholic Edition) and the Jerusalem Bible.

JANUARY

2 January, St Basil the Great and St Gregory Nazianzen

The two fourth century Greek doctors whom we celebrate today have a suitable location in the Calendar, coming as they do just after Christmas. Each made a notable contribution to the doctrine of the Incarnation.

St Basil suggested how the Incarnation reveals the whole Godhead. Because the God who lives and acts in three personally distinct ways is by nature one sole being, a knowledge of the Son must bring with it knowledge of the Father and of the Holy Spirit. Here, in the Incarnation, the three persons evidently move together: the Father willing, the Son carrying out his will, the Holy Spirit consolidating the result. So they do everywhere but not everywhere is their triune action openly disclosed. At Christmas this becomes, wonderfully, an open book for us.

St Gregory's contribution is concerned with explaining how in the saving work the entire Trinity ventured in the Incarnation it was necessary that the Son's humanity had to be truly complete. Only that is healed which is taken by the Word; only that is saved which is united to God. Our Lord was and is absolutely like us in all things save sin. Thus in redeeming us the incarnate God does not act upon us from without. Instead he lays hold of us in himself, and acts for us out of the inner depths of his co-existence with us. It is a sign of how in the Christian life that follows on from the Incarnation our existence is going to be *in him*.

These are profound lessons we need to ponder in Christmastide.

4 January, St Zedislava

Two days before the Epiphany, the feast of the manifestation of Christ to the nations, we read the Gospel of the call of Andrew and Peter. If we look at the broad sweep of Christian history we can see that this Scripture has been actualized in an amazing way.

From the mission of Andrew there comes Byzantine Christianity. Andrew is the patron of Constantinople; from him comes the

Christendom of the Greeks and the Slavs with its profound spirituality.

From the mission of Peter comes Western Christendom. Peter is the patron of Rome. From him comes eventually the extraordinary expansion of the Christianity of the West, from the Renaissance onwards, into continents newly discovered by Europeans or at least newly explored by them.

In each of these cases, Eastern and Western Christianity, we see how the Gospel has the power to put forth a whole culture or cultures, to express itself in literature and art, in ethics and customs, in theology and philosophy. This whole history witnesses to the power of the Incarnation, the new thing that came into the world at the first Christmas when the Word of God took human flesh.

Today's saint, Zedislava of Moravia, was born in a part of Europe where the waves of Eastern and Western Christianity met and mingled. Born about the time the Order of Preachers was founded, she was caught up in the religious revival it brought to the Czech lands. She excelled as a Christian wife and mother and, along with her husband, built up the Order in its three main branches; the friars, the enclosed nuns and the tertiaries living in the world. She created her own charity, a network to bring food to the sick poor whom she also served with her own hands. 'Christendom' would not be more than an imposing show unless the faith that underlies the culture of the Incarnation was embodied and lived out in individual lives. This is why the saints are important for us.

7 January, St Raymund of Peñafort

St Raymund was a Catalan born around 1180. By training a lawyer, he had risen to be archdeacon of Barcelona before abandoning a promising ecclesiastical career to become a friar. He proved a very God-centred one, a great lover of solitude, and also a zealous one, keen to bring not only heretics but Jews and Muslims into the Church. Serving the Word in both contemplation and action, he was thought worthy to be elected Master of the Dominicans in 1238.

Yet he remained a lawyer, and probably the single most influential lawyer in the history of the Western church since his collection of the 'decretals', as the canonical texts were known, remained standard until the codification of the canons of the Latin church in 1917. Was it a distraction from higher aims? I should say not. If the Church as a mystery of communion is not to remain at the level of vague abstraction it must be possible to spell out both the privileges and the demands of belonging to that communion. This is what canonists seek to do. To invest one's Christian discipleship in a lifelong pursuit of this question, governed by the great biblical virtues — indeed, divine attributes — of justice and mercy, is no contemptible thing. It is one example of that rigorous seeking of the will of God in which all holiness consists.

13 January, St Hilary

Hilary of Poitiers worked as a bishop in central Gaul — what we now call 'France' — in the mid fourth century. He was brought up as a pagan but read himself into the Church, being baptized when he was around thirty-five. Unfortunately, his becoming a Catholic Christian coincided with one of the worst crises the Church has known: the Arian crisis, which turned on whether or not Jesus Christ was really divine. Obviously, if Jesus Christ is not divine, then the message of the Church becomes a different one. It is no longer possible to say that in him, the Church's Founder, God acted directly and personally, intervening immediately in this world to reveal his own nature and change the conditions of our human existence so that sin and death, moral evil and the death of our bodily life, are no longer, as they used to be, invincible things.

Hilary saw this so clearly that when after only three years from his Baptism he was made a bishop, he determined to spend the rest of his life teaching and writing in defence of the divinity of our Lord. Because he was the main defender in the West of the Godhead of the Son — the 'Athanasius of the West' — and because this belief is so key to the whole framework of our understanding, the University of Oxford has honoured his memory by calling its Lent term after him and starting 'Hilary Term' each year on his day.

Hilary died before he could see the whole Church accept his teaching, which it did in 381 at the Second Ecumenical Council. Yet he never gave up. We too may not live to see orthodox Christianity once again becoming central to our culture. Like Hilary we must stick at it, keep faithful, and by word and example prepare the way.

17 January, St Anthony of Egypt

One day in the year 269 the son of well-to-do Egyptian farmers heard in the Liturgy the words of Jesus, 'If you would be perfect, go, sell all you have and give to the poor, and you will have treasure in heaven, and come, follow me'. Anthony interpreted those words in a particular way: in a literal way which (as so often) means a radical way, and a total way which (also as often) means a fruitful way.

As a consequence he became the father not just of his own soul, or the spiritual father of the various people who came to learn from him and share his way of life, but the patriarch of all monks: the father of monasticism, the father of all 'Religious life' or 'consecrated life' in the Church.

Was he really the very first person ever to have felt the call to abandon personal possessions for the sake of the Gospel, to embrace virginity for the sake of Christ, and to want to practice complete obedience to the Holy Spirit via a Rule of life? No, there were already Christian celibates and ascetics before him, but in none of them did monastic life become a clear programme with an obvious potential that commended itself to the episcopate, the pastors of the Church.

In the Book of the Apocalypse, St John knows of the existence of Christian virgins, but he didn't write an encomium on them; some of the Apostolic Fathers and the early Apologists knew that in the churches there were people who had left everything for the Lord, but they only give them a passing greeting or an occasional reference. On the other hand, St Athanasius took time off from saving the Church's faith in the divinity of Christ and governing the largest diocese in the early Christian world, so as to write a biography of St Anthony which is meant to show what the monastic life can be and is for the good of the Church.

And what is it, then? As found in Anthony, it is a single-minded seeking of the face of God, uncomplicated by family, property, career. Crucially, it involves a confrontation with the unredeemed sides to oneself, which are to be brought into captivity to Christ, as well as docility to the gracious initiatives of God in the life of the soul. Solitude is essential to it, but so also is brotherhood—the recognition of fellow-seekers. It can be a hidden life, but it can also constitute a dedicated resource for the Church's mission, a sort of spiritual fifth column, on whom the Church can confer tasks of various kinds. It is a dangerous way of life because, abandoning much that keeps people ticking over in a more or less sane and happy way, if it goes wrong it is disastrous. Few people are more to be pitied than a Religious who has ceased to seek God. But if it goes right, it is an icon of the Kingdom, the life of the sons and daughters of God, and among the most eloquent the Church has known.

21 January, St Agnes

St Agnes is one of the Italian girl martyrs of the fourth century persecutions. The sources describe her as a thirteen year old who refused marriage owing to her dedication to Christ. Like St Maria Goretti sixteen hundred years later, she preferred death to any violation of her virginity. Denounced to the State authority she was executed by the piercing of the throat.

The combination of supernatural faith with innocence is, we can speculate, peculiarly aggravating to the evil powers as it is likewise to their corresponding impulses in ourselves: the total caboodle we call 'the world, the flesh and the devil'. Conversely, the Church regards that combination—supernatural faith with innocence—as especially blessed. Sexual integrity of Agnes's kind is a sort of natural holiness which lets supernatural grace gain a firmer hold on the person, and through that person on the social continuum in which we are all inter-locked from birth. So the virgin martyr is someone special.

This is recognized symbolically in the moving ceremony carried out on this day every year at Rome. In the basilica of St Agnes, while the choir sings the antiphon *Stans a dextris eius Agnus nive candidior*, 'On her right stands a Lamb whiter than snow', two white lambs are brought into the sanctuary, blessed by the pope and then cared for until shearing time. From their wool is woven the pallia or triangular stoles sent to metropolitans, bishops of major sees, throughout the Western church as a sign of their hierarchical communion with the Church's centre.

Decoded, this custom is a statement that power and authority in the Church are, for their fruitful exercise, radically dependent on humility, integrity, and true innocence: on, in fact, the human responsiveness to God as Creator and Redeemer that St Agnes displayed.

24 January, St Francis de Sales

Francis de Sales ought to be an easy saint to appreciate, this sixteenth century bishop of Geneva who never saw his episcopal city owing to its takeover by Calvin. He was gentle, kind, sweet-tempered, warm-hearted, unfailingly courteous and gracious. No wonder he is known as 'the gentleman saint'.

When his friends asked him to write an *Introduction to the Devout Life*, he soon scrapped his original idea of a treatise on the ten commandments. Instead he would write about charity, how it is born, how it grows, how it comes to perfection. His other famous book was called simply *The Treatise on the Love of God*, and its title states exactly what it is about. So he is, it would seem, an easy saint to appreciate.

How was it done, though? This isn't Little Lord Fauntleroy living in the lap of luxury and always able to be amiable because he only had to raise a languid finger to have what he wanted. This was someone who only just escaped assassination several times during the French Wars of Religion. A great athlete makes terrific physical feats look like child's play. But we know they're not. To be able to do them means taking a lot of punishment first.

Nobody now opens St Francis' first effort at communication. Called *The Standard of the Holy Cross*, it claims to be a defence of the Catholic practice of venerating the crucifix over against Reformation-period iconoclasts. But its wider message is that only the Cross can symbolize Christianity. The Cross tells us how much the redemption of the human race cost the Saviour. It reveals the depth of human malice, the extent of our depravity, the force of our egoism. The Goodness by which all good things are good we nailed to a tree.

This explains why some students of his teaching find it extreme. Love always is, no matter what happens. That is not normally, I think, part and parcel of the code of a 'gentleman'. Gentlemen, surely, would scratch their heads at it. Yes, Francis de Sales is a difficult saint to understand.

25 January, The Conversion of St Paul

St Paul was a Jew of the Diaspora, the Dispersion, not a Palestinian Jew from the Holy Land itself, and was born close to what is now the border of Turkey and Syria. He had gone to Jerusalem to study Torah, the Law, with the great rabbi Gamaliel, and it was there that he heard of the infant Church, a new community which professed a new way of understanding the Word of God: a new faith, in effect, which did not put the Torah at the centre but instead put there Jesus, claimed to be the Messiah, crucified and risen, and accepted by God for the forgiveness of sins and the transformation of human beings into the divine image.

As a zealous Jew, Paul considered this message scandalous, and felt it a duty to eradicate Christianity not only in Jerusalem but outside it too. Hence his journey to Damascus. On the road, Jesus Christ made him his own. It is the first great conversion narrative of Christian history, and it was crucial for Paul's message: his Gospel of the righteousness of God which has now been disclosed to Christian faith as God's faithfulness to his own promises to Israel. He has shown the mercy promised the fathers, since while we were still sinners his Son, the Messiah, died for us.

In the Cappella Paolina in Rome, Michelangelo has a fresco which depicts the conversion scene: a powerfully built man (though in his letters Paul implies his physical appearance was unimpressive) suddenly reduced to the helplessness of a child.

Paul is lying on the ground pawing at his eyes as the accompanying guards and horses look on in dismay.

The words Paul heard spoken at this moment, 'I am Jesus whom you are persecuting', were unexpected, to say the least. The body Paul had attacked was the infant Church. But the Head of that body, living in it, communicating through it, was Christ. Paul's mature doctrine of the Church as the body of Christ the Mystical Body, later generations would call it, arises from this moment of revelation, illumination and vocation. In the era of the Word incarnate, the Church is the organism of God's presence to the world.

Hence the importance of the unity of the Church, a theme which also belongs to this season, since the week leading up to this feast is the octave of prayer for the reunion of Christians. Not, note, the reunion of the Church! In the Creed we profess that the Church is essentially one. That she cannot lose this essential unity follows from Paul's discovery that she is the Mystical Body of the Lord: 'mystical' not because the real Church is invisible but because she takes her rise from the mystery of Christ. We prayed over the past week (and I hope, not just then) that all those groups of Christians or individual Christians who are in some respect estranged from that unity should embrace it in its fullness. St Paul would have understood that.

26 January, St Timothy and St Titus

Who were Timothy and Titus? The liturgical books call them 'bishops' which is only a rough approximation. Basically, Timothy and Titus were regional vicars of the apostles, co-opted by them, more specifically by St Paul, as junior assistants who would continue the tasks of the apostolic ministry.

This was necessary at a time when those of the apostles who were still alive were conscious of growing old and feeble if one can imagine Paul as ever feeble. The specific functions of Timothy and Titus, over and above their general duty to imitate the apostle in his Christ-like way of life, were twofold, as we can see from St Paul's surviving letters to them. They were to guard the deposit of faith—the truths of revelation, together with the sacraments and

Christian morality. And they were to ordain local ministers: presbyters (priests) who would preside over the common life of local communities.

These two functions are still in Catholic Christianity the functions which distinguish a bishop from a presbyter, for a bishop is a guardian of the Gospel tradition and a provider of priests whom he ordains to share in, without fully reproducing, his own office as a vicar of the apostles, all on the model of today's saints.

Today's commemoration is important for showing the New Testament foundation of our specifically Catholic version of the Christian faith, according to which the apostolic preaching and ministerial succession continue in the sacramental life of the Church. St Timothy and St Titus are there to remind Christians generally that it is an *episcopally ordered Christendom in the apostolic succession* that carries forward in history the mandate entrusted to the holy apostles by the Lord himself.

28 January, St Thomas Aquinas

Thomas Aquinas was that rather rare thing, a saint canonized for the quality of their thinking. The motive force behind his canonization was the conviction of the pope, John XXII, that the Church would be illuminated by Thomas's lucid, luminous, presentation of Catholic doctrine. So the Church needed to say in public how highly she thought of his mind in its wisdom.

This doesn't mean the pope simply wanted to canonize Thomas for having a megawatt intelligence which, taken by itself, would not be a ground for asserting sanctity at all. Rather, the pope was convinced by the canonisation enquiry that Thomas's great mind was utterly in love with almighty God. But just because Thomas's mind was, in that way, a marvellous mind, the products of that mind his various writings could be, then, a mighty instrument for spreading the Catholic faith and getting people to understand it and appreciate it in something of the way Thomas had.

So the reason for venerating Thomas as a saint seems bound up with the reason for studying him as a theologian. The harmony, completeness and God-centredness of his teaching are remarkable. Likewise the way he integrated philosophy and doctrine, spiritu-

ality and theology, revelation and ethics. We certainly need to learn
from him how to see the Catholic faith as the most comprehensive
truth, beauty and goodness, able to invigorate all life and culture
because it comes from God—the God who, as Chesterton
remarked, is so much younger than we shall ever be.

And yet... For there is a 'yet' here, and a big one. If one looks
at the primitive lives of St Thomas, a very different story emerges.
Without denying his great wisdom (they compare him to Moses
on Sinai, 'aloft on the mountain of contemplation', and to Solomon
whose wisdom embraced everything from the towering cedars of
Lebanon to a hyssop plant in the crevice of a wall), the chief
emphasis of the early lives falls on Thomas' devotion. Devotion to
the incarnate Lord, to Christ crucified, and to the Blessed Eucharist
as the Body of him who took flesh from the Virgin and suffered
for all mankind: this came a resounding first in Thomas' life. One
has only to consider the words with which he greeted the sacrament when it was brought to him by the monks of Fossanova as
he lay dying: 'O price of my redemption and food for my pilgrimage, I receive you. For your sake have I studied and toiled and kept
vigil. I have preached you and taught you'. Note especially the
words, 'For your sake I have studied.' Could his writings have
been so fruitful for the Church if the motivation had been anything
other than this? 'Consider the power of the prayers of this holy
teacher', says one such life. 'They taught him understanding of
mysteries; they brought him all he desired'.

Thomas, as it were, put his finger, so the early lives say, on the
wound in Christ's side. This means, they explain, 'entering the side
of Christ as one invited and therein searching out and expressing
the mysteries contained there, with such assurance that it is as if
his hands had handled what the finger of his intellect pointed to'.

One could use the same comparison and say, The hand with
which, by the contact of faith, Thomas touched (or indicated) the
wound in the side of the crucified and risen Lord, this was the hand
with which he wrote the works that gained him the title *divus
Thomas*, 'St Thomas the Divine'. And gained him likewise our
desire to seek now the support of his prayer.

31 January, St John Bosco

John Bosco was born in 1815, the youngest son of a North Italian peasant who died when the child was two. He entered seminary when he was sixteen, his clothes and shoes provided by charity. His life work was education and an apostolate among adolescents, especially those of the new industrial working class.

John Bosco's method involved creating training workshops for destitute or unemployed youths with hostels attached for them to live in (I have seen one of these set-ups at Adwa, in Tigray, which is north-eastern Ethiopia). But this was no mere social outreach: the heart of each set-up was the oratory with the Mass, preaching and music.

The natural and the supernatural were carefully integrated. On Sundays, John Bosco took his boys to a country church for Mass, followed by breakfast and open-air games, and then a picnic lunch, after which the catechism was taught, with Vespers to finish.

Bosco's miracles are the best attested of modern times. He was a God-inebriated person whose preternatural gifts left intact a thoroughly practical intelligence. Characteristically, for all he touched succeeded, the Order for pastoral work he founded is now, I gather, the largest Order for men in the Western Church. When St John Bosco died, forty thousand people came to do homage to his body. They understood that for the Church a great person is a God-filled person and a sacrificial person. A saint can be nothing else, since he or she is in the image and likeness of Christ.

FEBRUARY

2 February, The Presentation of the Lord (1)

This is one of those feasts that somewhat confusingly have several names. First of all, there's what our mediaeval and early modern forebears would have called it, The Purification of our Lady. That is its most biblical name, and indeed its most Jewish name. Old Testament law prescribed a ritual purification for the mother so many days after childbirth (thirty-three for a girl, sixty-six for a boy). Until then she could touch nothing sacred, because childbirth is so awe-inspiring an event that it put the mother in a sort of limbo. In this sense—a subtle one—childbirth made her 'impure'.

But of course at this festival it is no ordinary mother coming to be purified. It is the all-pure Virgin who as the Mother of God is the way by which holiness itself, Jesus Christ, the Holy One of God, comes into the world. The role of Simeon and Anna but especially Simeon is to draw attention to the uniqueness of this particular act of purification by interpreting it through prophecy.

And so we come to the name of the feast in the Eastern church: 'The Meeting of the Lord with Simeon'. One of the great liturgical poets of the Greek church, St Andrew of Crete, wrote:

> Today the blessed Mother who is even holier than the Temple came into the Temple, and so showed to the world the world's Sustainer and Lawgiver. Old Simeon took him in his arms and to honour him cried out, 'Now let your servant go in peace for my eyes have seen your salvation'.

So there is here a manifestation, an epiphany, of the Saviour, which is why in a sense today is the last feast of Christmas, a detached free-floating piece of Christmastide.

There is in fact a *presentation* and so now we reach the contemporary name of this celebration in our Western calendars. By the Jewish Law, sacrificial gifts were presented to the Temple clergy so as to 'redeem' (that is, to buy back) the first-born, who otherwise was regarded as the property of God. Jesus, however, is not so much 'bought back' as entirely made over to the Father to whom he belongs not just as a human first-born but, more profoundly, as in his divine nature the only-begotten Son of the Father, not created but generated, 'loved into being' as Father Herbert McCabe used to put it, from before all time.

Like all feasts of light in winter darkness, today has gathered to itself a lot of popular devotion. You can see that from the popular names: Candlemas or in French *La Chandeleur*, the feast of candles, or in German *Mariälichtmesse*, 'Mary's Mass of light'. This Child will be a light to the Gentiles and the glory of his people Israel.

Yet today's feast would not be a fully Christian festival unless it also bore some relation to Easter as well as Christmas. By prophesying that Jesus will be a sign of contradiction, and that a sword of sorrow will pierce his mother's heart, Simeon shows what that relation is. He proclaims Jesus as the Messiah, but in a way that prefigures another presentation, another offering, the Oblation of the Cross.

2 February, The Presentation of the Lord (2)

So Simeon greets the messianic Child as not only the glory of his people Israel but also as a light to enlighten all the other peoples of the world. It's an anticipation of what Jesus will say of himself in the Gospel according to St John, 'I am the light of the world'.

This is one important way in which we confess the universal significance of Jesus Christ. A longing for illumination is found in every sphere of human life. There's a basic demand to be able to see, to have some kind of insight. Jesus claims that to see anything, anyone, any human achievement, for what it really is, we need to see it in his light. That is how we shall get a sense of perspective.

So the words of Simeon are in this light (as one might say!) the first Credo, the first Creed. All light is concentrated here in this Child, all light shines out from him. Jesus Christ is not just someone who said and did some illuminating things. He is *Lumen de Lumine*: Light from Light, true God from true God.

3 February, St Blaise

St Blaise is a fourth century martyr who hailed from Armenia which, as is fairly well known, was the first country in the world to accept Christianity as its official religion.

In Blaise's day, however, most of Armenia had been annexed to the Roman empire and that was still a pagan Rome, and a sporadically persecuting Rome at that.

His legend which like all legends surely starts out from some historical memory, on the good old principle, 'no smoke without fire', is an attractive one. He was already a bishop when persecution broke out, whereupon he took refuge in a cave. To us, hiding in caves sounds like a schoolboy game. But many people in the world live in caves. I myself have seen some, in the highlands of Ethiopia.

Living in his cave, then, Blaise discovered he had a gift for healing sick or wounded animals, which naturally enough made him very popular among the locals. His reputation was clinched when he saved a boy from choking on a fishbone. The boy's mother thanked the bishop by a gift of food and candles. That incident is the origin of the traditional blessing of throats on St Blaise's day.

In the Western Middle Ages Blaise emerged as a much sought after intercessory saint, one of the so-called Fourteen Holy Helpers, whose collective expertise in healing diseases of various kinds made them a sort of heavenly International Health Service, the HINHS. In England, and specifically in East Anglia, his cult survived the Reformation here and there in unofficial form. Parson Woodforde the diarist describes a procession by Norwich townspeople in his honour in 1783. I think we have to say that is an extraordinary survival in a Church which had suppressed, with State assistance, the cult of saints, and an eloquent testimony to how long the memory of Blaise's benevolence lingered.

4 February, St Catherine dei Ricci

Alessandra Lucrezia Romola dei Ricci (in religion she took the name 'Catherine' in honour of her better-known fellow-Dominican Catherine of Siena) was a sixteenth century Italian nun, born in 1522 into a wealthy Florentine family connected by banking and political interests to the Medici, the ruling house of the city. She went to school with Benedictine women who ran a rather relaxed and civilized establishment, religious enough to awaken Alessandra's sensibilities in that direction but not austere enough to satisfy them. Outside Florence, at Prato, however, was the Dominican monastery of San Vincenzo, noted for its strictness of observance, and thither she went.

Her behaviour in the novitiate was disappointing. She was dozy and droopy at recreation, late for Office and Mass (if she got there at all), and only with great difficulty was she accepted for profession. Later it transpired she was in receipt of mystical graces that left her drained of energy. After profession, her ecstasies became more prolonged, along with visions and locutions of Christ, his Mother and the saints, and, above all, the stigmata which she received at Easter 1542. She became a celebrated and much sought out figure, the object of a stream of visitors and gawpers, to save her from which her Community, with much misgiving, gave her administrative tasks as sub-prioress. She could now have the excuse that she was too busy to see people.

It was then that she discovered her real talent for government and spiritual direction. In 1552 she was unanimously elected prioress and continued to be re-elected for thirty-six years, during which time she acquired a large number of directees including two future popes: Marcellus III and Clement VIII. Many letters survive from such correspondence.

Her secret lay in combining vigour with sweetness. If a nun was not in choir she would go and find her and escort her to her stall. But that evening she would call at the miscreant's room and say some kind word. Similarly with her directees: to one man whom she thought was fasting excessively she sent a basket of food with a note, 'We must not die but live and do good so as to give God glory and honour.'

One of her last acts was to put into the furnace of the monastery kitchen a set of papers the nuns had collected as testimonies to her holiness. On her deathbed she underwent the event the Eastern church calls transfiguration by the Uncreated Light. This is a saint who should be better known.

5 February, St Agatha

St Agatha is a figure partly obscured by the mists of time. She comes towards us from the age which succeeded the apostles and, on their foundation, was sending forth the message of the Gospel in the words of the first Fathers of the Church. After the peace of the Church, when the spasmodic imperial persecutions ceased, Agatha soon became a favourite figure to include when mosaic workers were commissioned to produce a visual equivalent of that message. And so she gazes out at us in, for example, that wonder-work of ancient Christianity, the basilica of Sant'Apollinare Nuovo at Ravenna. The poet Yeats, describing such mosaics, called their figures 'sages standing in God's holy fire'.

We know a few crucial things about her. She was Sicilian. She was an ascetic—someone who had consecrated herself to God in Christ as a virgin. And not merely after her vow but because of it, the finger of the persecuting authority pointed to her, and she became a martyr.

I don't think the connection between virginity and martyrdom is just by chance. A hedonistic, fairly decadent, society may be impressed when beautiful young women renounce the use of sex for religious reasons. Alternatively, such a society may be infuriated by it. It doesn't surprise me that local government officials in the late Roman empire handed over Agatha to a brother-keeper, even if the name 'Aphrodisia' given to this madame is obviously *faute de mieux*. What, if anything, does surprise me is the way critical historians are so sceptical of ancient accounts of martyrdom that pile on the agony. When the brothel treatment failed, say the Acts of Agatha's martyrdom, she was tortured by rods, rack and fire, before her breasts were cut off and she died in prison as a result of her injuries. Many historians consider this narrative excessive and therefore fictional. One wonders where they were living in the twentieth century, age of countless barbarities in war and terrorism, not to mention the occasional pathological acts of obscene violence committed by private persons against each other.

A few years ago, I was lucky enough to be given a ride on the Orient Express from London to Venice, and obviously it *was* an opportunity to re-read *Murder on the Orient Express* by another Agatha, Agatha Christie. Christie saw her detective stories (I quote from the authorised biography) as 'morality plays, demonstrating that there was wickedness in the world', and her biographer goes on to say that the second lesson of Agatha Christie's morality plays was that such wickedness 'could be found out and sin expiated'. If there is no such thing as wickedness, only moral feebleness, itself the result of social or psychological conditioning, then of course we don't need a religion of redemption, such as Christianity is. St Agatha's martyrdom compounded flagrant injustice with the offence of sacrilege, because as a consecrated virgin she was one of those who, in our Lord's words in St Luke's Gospel 'have chosen the better part and it shall not be taken from them'. It *was* taken from her, like life itself. Sheer wickedness.

But the saints repay malice with goodness, which is why St Gregory the Great did her the great honour of adding her to the carefully selected list of those who figure by name in the historic Eucharistic Prayer of the Church of the Roman rite. Let us honour her likewise.

6 February, St Paul Miki and his companions

The story of the Japanese martyrs bears a strange resemblance to that of the martyrs of the Iconoclast dispute in early Byzantium. Not that the Byzantine martyrs were killed for refusing to foreswear Christianity. On the contrary, they are the first examples of Orthodox Christians put to death by a State which claimed to share the same Orthodox faith. The comparison lies elsewhere. It lies in the way the Japanese authorities, in the persecution of the Church which broke out in the Japanese islands towards the end of the sixteenth century, made the fate of their victims turn on their willingness to desecrate the sacred images.

Each suspect was presented with an image of either the Mother and Child or Christ crucified and invited to tread it underfoot. Many refused even to touch the image with their toe, and thus confessed their faith, and paid the penalty.

There are today, I am told, many moving mementos of the hidden Church whose life persisted in the wake of this persecution, which coincided with the cutting off of Japan from the outside world. The mementos have their own version of iconic form. Some are mirrors with images of a Buddhist paradise on the reverse side. But when a light is shone through the mirror a silhouette appears: it is Christ on the Cross with our Lady praying at the Cross's foot.

Others are statuettes which seem to be of Buddhist deities, but a tiny almost invisible cross engraved on the back indicates this is the Virgin Mary, with Japanese features and disguised in a kimono.

Many of those who produced these images lived in the islands off the coastal region of Nagasaki where there are many remotely situated Catholic churches, including timber ones, from the nineteenth century. They witness not only to the concealed life the Japanese Catholic church led for three hundred years but also to its remarkable resurgence. There is a saying, 'The blood of the martyrs is the seed of the Church'. On today's feast we can see its truth.

7 February, The Departed Parents of Members of the Order of Preachers

Piety towards one's dead parents has been a major factor in the religious experience of mankind from China to ancient Rome. The urge to revere the memory of parents has been one of the nerves animating religion at large. Why is it important for us?

Pretty obviously, without my parents, I would not be here at all. So my parents are, and always will be, my primary link with the human race. This is how in my flesh, my bones, I am linked to all the generations of man as they come and go. This is how I received my basic inheritance of nature and nurture. Meditating on that saves me from thinking of myself as a self-made man who, as the old gibe about the English has it, worships his creator: i.e. himself.

So, what my parents have given me, not that it was perfect, is the fundamental form of receiving that I know. If I think about it, I realize that their relation to me makes me *a being that exists first and foremost by receiving*. In piety towards dead parents we recognize this fact and in doing so we give them all we can now give— homage, gratitude. A homage and gratitude as imperfect, no doubt, as was their gift to us. Original sin makes sure of that.

No life is without its regrets, says the king in Alan Bennett's play. But none is without its consolations. So what is our consolation here? One answer could be: the possibility of offering the Sacrifice of the Mass. The imperfect situation of receiving a flawed inheritance, and equally imperfectly giving thanks for it, is changed in the Mass by the offering of Christ. Here we are shown how the whole thing can be brought within a perfect receiving: Jesus' receiving from the Father, and a perfect giving back of thanks his self-giving to the Father. For in the Sacrifice of the Church, the Head, Christ, enables the Body, the Church, to participate in his own perfect 'Thank you' to the Father.

10 February, St Scholastica

We keep today the memorial of St Scholastica, sister of St Benedict, the patriarch of monks. Her portrayal by Gregory the Great in his 'Dialogues' on the life and miracles of her brother doesn't give us much sense of her personal distinctiveness. Nevertheless, she has functioned in the Western tradition as a kind of female Benedict, an archetype of the consecrated virgin.

Historically speaking, Benedict was not really the father of all monks. For one thing, he saw it as his task to pass on the wisdom of the monks of the East, the monastics who had preceded him in Syria and Egypt: mentioning especially how he had drawn inspiration from St Basil as well as from the sayings of the desert fathers. For another, there were many monks in the West before Benedict: in hermitages in Gaul, or clustering around the Roman basilicas, or again, in bishops' houses in North Africa. But Benedict somehow came to focus the wider monastic vocation with peculiar sharpness for the whole later Catholic Church.

On a smaller scale, something is true likewise of St Scholastica. She functions in a special symbolic way in the tradition of women's consecrated life.

St Gregory's appreciation of her is centred on her attentiveness to divine things and the prospect of heaven—communion with God, then—in the context of obedience to the word of God. He stresses her fervent and intelligent anticipation of the rewards of Gospel discipleship. Hers is a mind that has been re-trained by the willing study of God's word: her very name, 'Scholastica', suggest as much.

By the grace of God, Christian asceticism reverses the fall of Eve, the fall of Adam, which was their premature wanting to be like God, but not in God's time, and not in God's way. They refused to let God give them his gifts in the way he knew best. They made a unilateral declaration of independence from him and had to discover for themselves how, since we are made for communion with him, to choose against him leads inevitably to dust and ashes.

The Christian monastic resolves on single-minded and single-hearted obedience to the word of God, with the loving concentration of her or his powers. This, through grace, aligns them with the Saviour who did not presume on equality with God but humbled himself, taking on the form of a servant and being obedient even unto death. The Fall is reversed and in the life of charity Eden comes to be again in a new way, albeit in patches, even if highly significant patches like snowdrops as a sign of Spring.

11 February, Our Lady of Lourdes

Today's memorial, Our Lady of Lourdes, is unusual. The Church teaches that every Catholic is free to accept or to reject what are called 'private revelations': alleged visionary (or auditory) experiences of God, Christ, the Mother of the Lord, or the saints, which leave the visionary concerned with some special message to give to the Church. You can take them or you can leave them. Once the Church has ascertained that the supposed messages don't actually contradict her teaching, you can be sceptical or credulous about them, agnostic or convinced, reserve your judgment or be inclined to accept them. It's up to you.

The putative apparition of the Blessed Virgin Mary at Lourdes in the mid nineteenth century to an almost illiterate shepherdess later canonized as St Bernardette is in a class if not of its own then at least a class that has exceptionally few other members. It is a rare example of a devotion that has arisen from private revelation and yet has found its way into the calendar of the universal Church, there to be celebrated in and for itself. That seems to imply that, without actually forcing it upon us, the Church positively commends it to us, rather than, as would be normal, leaving it a purely open question.

The distinguished Edwardian priest-novelist Robert Hugh Benson, son of Archbishop Benson of Canterbury, wrote a good book about the shrine at Lourdes. Before he went there, his position could be described as neutral with a slight bias towards acceptance of its authenticity. Without much enthusiasm, he thought that what he called 'the supernatural hypothesis' was the most economical explanation for the apparent miracles and, in that degree, the most satisfactory one.

He came back with three convictions. First, the presence of our Lady was virtually tangible at Lourdes for any person of good will who had the Catholic faith. Secondly, Lourdes would be of enormous importance in vindicating the Church vis-à-vis science. The medical committee set up to investigate the cures, with its deliberate representation of agnostics and atheists, would in the nicest possible way teach science to know its place. Thirdly, more than any other phenomenon in the modern world, Lourdes would show people the continuing significance of the Incarnation. As God had once entered into matter in Jesus Christ, so now God continues to work to heal both souls and bodies.

And indeed, for the site of a private revelation, Lourdes is a remarkably public place. Lots of non-Catholics, and indeed non-Christians, know something about it, and the Church likes it like that.

The Church does not in fact say we *have to* accept that the Mother of God really appeared in that little town in the Pyrenees. But she does expect us not to be stand-offish towards the claim, much less dismissive of it. We should look at Lourdes not uncritically yet reverently, with the eyes of faith.

13 February, Blessed Jordan of Saxony

On the 13th of February 1237, the second Master of the Dominicans was drowned off Acre on the coast of Palestine. He had been an administrator and academic, a successful promoter of vocations, a director and a friend of enclosed nuns. Arguably, he did more than St Dominic in practice to establish the Order of Preachers as a synthesis of elements—study, asceticism, liturgy, fraternal living, preaching—all contained within a well thought out governmental frame.

Did being German have something to do with this? I imagine the qualities we associate with Germans—methodical, systematic, thorough-going—are a product of the educational reforms of early nineteenth century Prussia. Earlier, prominent Germans in Church history such as Eckhart, Luther, Boehme, were more like semi-crazed visionaries. Yet without a vision of some kind, no amount of planning and prudence will be of much use where Religious life is concerned.

Jordan's letters reveal that his vision was deeply and passionately Christological. The book we have to follow, he says, is no longer a rule book, useful and even indispensable as rules are. No, the book is the God-man, Jesus Christ, whom we can read like an open book on Calvary. There, as Jordan puts it, he: 'stretched out on the Cross like a parchment on which he has written with his bruises and which he has illuminated with his generous Blood'.

14 February, St Cyril and St Methodius

So today we have the feast of the blood brothers Methodius and Constantine, the latter of whom, later in life, when he became a monk, took the name Cyril. They were highly born and highly educated residents of ninth century Constantinople, where Constantine was the librarian of the great library of Hagia Sophia, the patriarchal church. But they came from Thessalonica, which in this period was half-Slav. So when the Byzantine emperor received a request from a local ruler in what is now Moravia, in the Czech Republic, to send some missionaries, his eye fell on them. And off they went.

They were hugely successful. So much so that they aroused the opposition of Frankish missionaries (Germans, we would now say) who, like the Byzantines, were also keen on being the first to convert the Slavonic peoples. This conflict was serious stuff. A synod of German bishops at Regensburg ordered St Methodius to be (let us put it politely) 'detained' in a monastery on an island in Lake Constance, where he remained for several years. Not only ecclesiastical but political influence over a vast area turned on which mission would win out.

It says a great deal for the papacy of the period that, despite the brothers' predominantly Eastern orientation in Liturgy, theology, spirituality, and (who can doubt it?) politics the popes supported Methodius and Constantine-Cyril and not their Western competitors.

Blessed John Paul II made them co-patrons of Europe shortly after he himself became pope. His aim was obvious: to balance the very Western figure of St Benedict with two figures who are treated as one because their missions were one. His decision anticipated a sometimes overlooked aspect of his pontificate, which was to appeal to the Christian East as a way of making good the weaknesses of the contemporary Christian West. More than half the references in the 1992 *Catechism of the Catholic Church* are to Oriental sources.

The pope's scheme was a challenge to Catholics who are overwhelmingly of the Latin rite: a challenge to us to recognize the parity of the Christian East in the making of the Catholic Church.

22 February, The Chair of Peter

Today's feast is an interesting example of the Christianisation of pagan customs. Around this date, the pagan Romans commemorated their dead relations. Roughly now was the *parentalia*, when food was brought to the graves of the dead and everyone had a party there. It sounds rather macabre to us, but presumably the spirit of it was something like the Irish 'wake' which is (I am told) a heady mixture of corpses and poteen. For the pagans, the day following the *parentalia* was kept as a celebration of surviving relatives — those who were still here despite the ravages of nature, time or human depravity. This was the *cara cognatio*, literally the 'dear ties of blood'.

Today's feast, the Chair of Peter, was introduced as a Christian substitute for the *cara cognatio*. It was a celebration of the head of the Church's family, by reference to whom all disciples are inter-related, the chief of the apostles: St Peter.

In the Christianised version, Peter was fêted more as a surviving relative, then, than as a dead one. Interesting, and there could be two explanations for it. First, for the Gospel religion, the most real connexion there can be between people is not the biological continuum. Instead, it is life in Christ. Since Peter lives in the risen Lord to whom he witnessed he is more alive than dead. But that could be said of course of anyone who died 'in Christ'.

So there is also, secondly, a further consideration more specific to St Peter, and this is the idea that Peter's role or office or spiritual authority as the *paterfamilias*, the head of the household, continues in his successor, the Roman bishop, the pope. This is one of the most continuously held convictions of the Roman church from the homilies of Leo the Great in the fifth century to Paul VI arriving in 1970 at Geneva to visit the World Council of Churches and introducing himself with the words, 'Nous sommes Pierre'. 'We are Peter.'

Today, then, we celebrate St Peter as still teaching in the living voice of his successors. We also celebrate, more widely, the abolition of the distinction between the dead and the living by the Resurrection of Christ to which Peter bore witness at the empty tomb and through the Easter appearances. And we pray that the clarity of doctrine which once rang out at his profession of faith at Caesarea Philippi, 'You are the Christ the Son of the living God', and earned him the headship of the apostolic fellowship, will always (and not only in making those rare *ex cathedra* judgments) be characteristic of those who sit on his Chair.

23 February, St Polycarp

Polycarp of Smyrna is one of the most important links between the holy apostles and the Fathers, and therefore a great witness to the continuity of the Gospel in the Church. His long life is part of the explanation. The contemporary account of his martyrdom testifies to it in his own words: 'For eighty-six years I have been his servant, and he has never done my wrong; how can I blaspheme my King who saved me?'

The Martyrdom of Polycarp is one of the most moving documents in its genre not least when it portrays how in effect he signed his own death warrant, offering (with perhaps a twinkle in his eye) to instruct his examiners in the illegal faith: 'If you wish to study the Christian doctrine, choose a day, and you will hear it.'

What good did it do? If today you go to the top of the hill, just behind Smyrna, where Polycarp was executed, no shrine meets your eye. The playground of a large secondary school now covers the spot. In a terrible act of revenge for the Greek invasion of Anatolia

in 1920, the Turks burned this chiefly Eastern Orthodox city to the
ground before repopulating it with their own. And yet Smyrna is
the only city of the old province of Roman Asia still to retain a
flourishing Christian and more specifically Catholic community.
But what shall we find when another nineteen hundred years have
passed?

The question of the fruits of martyrdom cannot be answered
with such specificity. All we can say is that the prayers and
sacrifices of the saints form an integral part of that government of
the world by which God carries out his Providential plan: preserv-
ing nature, bestowing grace, and integrating the whole through
the redemptive Incarnation which brings all things together under
one divine-human Head Jesus Christ, St Polycarp's 'King'.

MARCH

1 March, St David

Today's feast is a reminder that the part of the Catholic Church we live in is not the Catholic Church in England, but the Catholic Church in England *and Wales*—a country which was fully politically integrated with England in the year 1536, just in time for the Protestant Reformation. Christianity had entered Wales in the second century. Christian literature there goes back to the fifth century, and Wales is thought to have been completely Christianised by the end of the sixth century just when St Augustine, later called 'of Canterbury', was setting out from Rome to convert the pagan Anglo-Saxons.

St David belongs with the golden age of Welsh history, the so-called 'age of the saints'. Typically these were monastic saints in the tradition of the desert fathers: such men as Illtyd, Teilo, Dyfrig, Beuno, Samson, and David himself. The monastic colleges of the age of the saints attracted students from elsewhere in the Christian world. David himself, however, was not a professional teacher but an ascetic and a defender of the faith.

St David is portrayed as having two qualities that don't always go hand in hand. On the one hand, he is described in severely ascetic terms: a man who lived a highly mortified life, a lover of silence, a teetotaler (hence his nickname, David the Water-drinker'). On the other hand, in the doctrinal struggles of the time, he appears as a champion of the free grace of God, over against an heretical exaltation of the human will, Pelagianism. His austerity was not, then, a case of the will grinding down poor old battered human nature yet again. Instead, it was, evidently, the fruit of responsiveness to the philanthropy of God, to God's loving kindness towards man, which asks of us, appropriately, a like generosity in turn. In the words of the Passiontide hymn we shall soon be singing: 'Love so amazing, so divine/ demands my soul, my life, my all'.

7 March, St Perpetua and St Felicity

The Passion of St Perpetua and St Felicity is one of the most precious
documents to come down to us from the ancient Church. Its
heroines were arrested at Carthage, in North Africa, in 203. Felicity
was a slave, and was pregnant at the time of her arrest; she was
delivered of her child just before her martyrdom. Perpetua, by
contrast, was the wife of a man of some standing in society. But
she too was a young mother, still nursing a baby at the breast. They
are known to us through their own words, telling of the visionary
experiences they had prior to their ordeal: visions of struggle, and
a dangerous climb, but also of drinking cool water and playing
like children.

Those confessions have been incorporated apparently by the
hand of an eye-witness into an account of their trial and execution,
which took the form of goring by bulls prior to piercing through
the throat by the sword.

They are merry martyrs. 'Thanks be to God', said Perpetua, as
she approached her martyrdom, 'that I was merry in the flesh so
am I still merrier here'. It's reminiscent of our own Thomas More's
passing up Tower Hill to the place of his martyrdom, as merry as
a bridegroom on the way to his wedding (so people reported).
Felicity was so relieved that her daughter was born in prison and
immediately adopted by a Christian: she had feared that as a
consequence of her pregnancy she would be spared and lose the
martyr's crown.

Is it conceivable that sane young women, looking forward to
motherhood, would die in such a spirit? It *is* conceivable to those
for whom revelation sets forth the banquet of salvation, surpassing
all other joys and endless in its festivity. We are the ones who
should be pitied if we cannot make head or tail of their priorities.

8 March, St Felix

Our Lady of Walsingham is the chief patron of the church of East
Anglia, but there are two secondary patrons, Edmund, king and
martyr and today's saint, Felix. Felix is the more obscure of the
two, unless you happen to live at Felixstowe, but he's also probably
the more crucial.

In 630 archbishop Honorius of Canterbury received news that the first in the line of Edmund's Christian predecessors, Sigebert, had returned from exile and was poised to reclaim these shires for himself and the faith. The primate at once asked a Burgundian bishop—this was Felix—to travel north with all speed, and take responsibility for one of those royal-stroke-episcopal collaborations that had proved so fruitful elsewhere in Anglo-Saxon England.

Felix settled at Dunwich, on the Suffolk coast, a place that has since disappeared into the North Sea. He gave priority to education, establishing a school described as being on the Gaulish model, which implies it was a precursor of the far more elaborate cathedral schools of the high Middle Ages: teaching the basics of a liberal education with some philosophy and theology as well.

St Felix also founded the monastery of Soham near Cambridge where he was buried, until his relics were translated to Ramsey Abbey.

He was a spiritual exile, among a largely pagan people. Just as we are now.

17 March, St Patrick

We celebrate today one of the greatest of the early British saints. St Patrick was probably a Strathclyde Briton, born about 385 near what is now Glasgow. His mother tongue would have been a form of Welsh, but since his father was not only a deacon of the Church but also a minor civil servant in the rapidly dissolving Roman empire of the West, Patrick was brought up to write in Latin.

His connexion with Ireland, then entirely pagan, was fortuitous. He was captured by Irish pirates and sold into slavery. At this stage of his life his principal aim, not unnaturally, was to escape. But when he succeeded and got back home, he heard on his inner ear the voices of the Irish pleading to him to return and teach them the faith.

Ordained in Gaul, he was consecrated as bishop for the Irish and from his centre at Armagh carried out very effective missionary journeys. St Patrick is not only the greatest missionary Britain has produced, with the possible exception of St Boniface. He also provided the model which, in time, in the ninth century and then again in the nineteenth and twentieth centuries, made the Irish church itself the greatest missionary church in Europe. In the modern period, what made that possible was, in a sense, the British empire, in the way it spread through the world the English language—a language wholly unknown of course in either Britain or Ireland in Patrick's lifetime. Of such twists and turns is history made.

What remains constant is the truth exemplified by St Patrick's career: one lamp lights another. That should encourage us in our own efforts to spread the faith by using whatever gifts we have. The judgment of history, fortunately, is not ours but God's.

19 March, Solemnity of St Joseph (1)

Today's feast is called the solemnity of Joseph the Husband of Mary. But the title given to Joseph in the Gospels is not actually the 'husband of Mary' though, to be sure, he is also described as that. His title, however, is 'Joseph, son of David': Joseph, descendant of king David, heir of the ancient Israelite royal family to whom, according to the Jewish hope, the promised Messiah would belong. St Matthew's Gospel, where this appears, is often said to be the most Jewish of the Gospels and certainly it is so in the way it presents St Joseph as the son of David.

Indeed, if the Babe of Bethlehem came into this world in the way indicated by this Gospel, namely, as the child of a Virgin Mother, then St Matthew had above all, for Jewish readers a problem on his hands. How could Jesus be God's Messiah if he were not descended in the male line from David, of whose lineage the Messiah would be born? Joseph's adoption of Jesus, his foster-fathering him, means for Mathew that Joseph can pass on to Jesus his own title, son of David, the title the crowds will give our Lord as he enters Jerusalem on the first Palm Sunday to claim his inheritance: 'Hosanna to the Son of David!'

St Joseph is, then, necessary to the Gospel because, as the legal father of this Child, he guarantees the authenticity of Jesus in Jewish eyes. He stands for, and protects, the Jewishness of Jesus in his Davidic claim. And this is vital. Only if Jesus is the Jewish Messiah can he be the promised Mediator between man and God,

since only the Jewish people knew the one true God for who he
really is. As St John's Gospel has it, 'Salvation comes from the Jews'
that is to say, it comes via the Jews—via their history and experience which until Jesus were the only fully medium for knowing
the one and only God.

That is the claim we also make for Israel as Christians by
binding the Jewish Old Testament with our own New Testament
into a single book, the Bible. Though paganism may have occasional happy guesses and correct intuitions of the truth, the golden
line of the special revelation of the Creator of the human race to
his human creatures runs through the history of Israel, and
nowhere else.

Today's Solemnity, then, reminds us of the Church's debt to
Judaism. It reminds us of the continuing validity for us of the Old
Testament and the respect and reverence and curiosity which the
Old Testament should awaken in us. It reminds us of the rock from
which we were hewn. It reminds us that as Gentile Christians we
are only, in St Paul's words, a 'wild olive branch' grafted onto the
stock of Israel. It reminds us of the special place within the Church
of Catholics of Jewish descent. It reminds us, finally, of our
obligations to the community of believing Jews who still hope as
we do, notably in Advent, for the final coming of the Messiah even
though they do not know he has come once and his name is Jesus.

19 March, Solemnity of St Joseph (2)

St Joseph has his unique place in the Gospels, just as our Lady, the
Baptist and the apostles have theirs. His presence—active and
vigilant—is pervasive in the narratives of the Infancy of Christ.

Joseph is entrusted with very specific tasks: to make ready the
birth of the Child; to name him, and to protect him against the
hostile forces of the environing world. After that, he would seem
to withdraw, so as to clear the way for the revelation of the eternal
Father, whose proxy in the life of this baby he has been.

And yet the 'economy' of this saint, the dispensation of Providence of which Joseph was the subject, is not exhausted when the
hidden years come. It is, in the first instance, through Joseph that
the Lord Jesus, according to his humanity, experiences the love of

the heavenly Father as artworks showing the holy Child in the arms of St Joseph seek to indicate.

That implies St Joseph had some exceptional qualities or at any rate some exceptional version of ordinary paternal qualities. In the writings of the so-called 'French School', outstanding masters of spiritual theology in seventeenth century France, Joseph and Mary are described as the 'oratory' where the Only-Begotten Son, now a member of our race, re-finds the Father in the Holy Spirit. One of its members, Jean-Jacques Olier, wrote: 'The admirable St Joseph was given to the earth to express the adorable perfection of God the Father in a tangible way. In his person alone, he carried the beauties of God the Father, his purity and love, his wisdom and prudence, his mercy and compassion. One saint alone is destined to represent God the Father, whereas an infinite number of creatures, a multitude of saints, are needed to represent Jesus Christ.'

We talk of the hidden life of our Lord in the home at Nazareth, which spans the years between the Infancy Gospels and the Baptism of Christ. For Olier's colleague in that School, Bishop Bossuet, while Jesus showed himself to the apostles in order to be proclaimed to the world, he showed himself to St Joseph so as to be hidden, so as to be enclosed in this family circle. The obscurity that human beings tend to fear (just see how nowadays people want to be celebrities!) was chosen at Nazareth by One who was personally God.

And it would be chosen by him again on Calvary, when he died as one of countless victims of religious intolerance and State injustice, outside the City wall. The fruitfulness of hiddenness and willing solidarity with those who suffer: this is all part of our message to the modern world.

25 March, Solemnity of the Annunciation of the Lord (1)

Every great feast has its grace: most obviously Christmas, Easter, Pentecost. Each has its own particular blessing for our lives. This remark may seem a mere devotional flourish, but it is in fact theologically well-founded. Each such feast brings to the Church's mind an act of God, and each of God's actions tells us something of what God is like. And when we have before us some additional disclosure of what God is like, then we are invited to respond to him, to let him into our lives, *in the very way* he shows us there. So at Christmas we meet God as a child, the innocence of God; at Easter we meet God as a crucified human being, the love of God, suffering and victorious; at Pentecost we meet God as Holy Spirit, the power of God taking hold of the apostles and sending them out to proclaim their faith to the world.

What, then, is the special grace of today's feast, the Annunciation of the Lord? To borrow a phrase from Hilaire Belloc, it seems to be the *courtesy* of God. God's plan of salvation for mankind turned at its most crucial point on whether or not Mary, out of her own freedom, would say 'Yes': whether or not she would consent to what her Maker asked her, and he asked a simply enormous thing: whether she would let her whole being be given over, now and for ever, to a relation with his Son. She was to be not only the mother of the Son but his 'dear companion', his *alma socia*, as the Latin theological tradition calls her. Henceforth she would live her life exclusively as his Mother and his Bride. But only if she gave the word.

We see this courtesy of God in more diffuse form at various points. We see it in nature, in the growth of crops and the yield of the sea. These are gifts of God which, if we wish, we can take as they are, without adverting to God and thinking no more about it. Or alternatively we can make out behind these gifts the Giver himself.

Again, courtesy is built into the act of specifically Christian faith. God does not force himself upon us. He invites us, courteously, to recognize his Incarnation from the signs he gives us in the Gospels and elsewhere. We can see the same attribute in act in the way Jesus makes disciples: he calls them and there is something commanding about it—it is an imperative, yes but what he asks them to take upon them is his 'sweet [or 'gentle'] yoke'. And he predicts that from the Cross he will *draw* all men to himself, attract them by the spectacle of One who is consubstantial with their Creator dying for love of them.

On today's Solemnity, then, we pray that the blessing of the Annunciation mystery will pour out on all the Church: a deeper discovery of God's gentleness and tact, and, from our side, a more

adequate response to the courtesy of God who on this day took
our human flesh for ever as the New Adam thanks to the perfect
response to his courtesy on the part of Mary, the New Eve.

25 March, Solemnity of the Annunciation of the Lord (2)

Today's Solemnity celebrates the beginning of the Incarnation. It
is the moment when by his Spirit the eternal God fertilized an
ovum in the womb of the Virgin Mary and united that embryonic
example of human nature to the person of his eternal and only-
begotten Word.

So it's an event at once biological and theological, and therefore
rather shocking to us. On the whole, people like to keep God at a
certain distance where we are safe from him, safe from his
demands, safe to get on with our own lives. But no, he came very
close, shockingly close. He entered the human race as a foetus, like
the foetuses we throw away every day into the incinerators of our
hospitals and clinics. He became a human being as we are, and
vulnerable, therefore, to the worst we could do to him. In this sense,
the Annunciation points ahead to the Crucifixion, which was our
last word to God's only Son in this world. Beyond that there lies
only the Resurrection which will be God's last word to us.

Because the Annunciation is the beginning of the Incarnation,
today's festival has been declared in recent times a feast of the
Lord, a feast of Christ himself. Previously, it was a feast of our
Lady, 'Lady Day' as the mediaeval English called it. It's easy to see
why a change was made in the way the Calendar describes this
Solemnity, but it's also easy to see why the accent has in other
periods been placed differently: placed on the Mother of God.

God acts, but man must allow God's action to unfold. Grace
comes first but in our freedom we must receive the grace of God,
receive the God of grace, into our lives. Humanly speaking,
without Mary's consent to the Incarnation, the entire plan—the
strategy of God to save us—would have come unstuck. Unless
Mary was prepared to turn her life upside down, to move towards
whatever unknown future he was leading her to, he could not have
become man, and we would not be saved.

When the Fathers, and later spiritual writers, thought of Mary's words to the angel, 'Be it done to me according to thy word', they took them to be the disclosure of Mary's inner life, her basic attitude to God, and the model, too, for the way we ourselves should live. There, in her openness and receptivity to God, is the secret of spiritual living. It's no use just being thankful to God when things go our way. We have to accept him in the whole package of his Providence. Even in things that hurt and humiliate us, that set us back, we have to see his loveable will. The humiliation may be bitter, but if we can see and love his will in it, there is at least a chance we shall grow greater not smaller by means of it. Until the end Mary's song was *Magnificat*. 'My soul magnifies the Lord.'

25 March, Solemnity of the Annunciation of the Lord (3)

Today's Gospel presents us with one of the miracles that are built into the structure of our religion: the virginal conception of Jesus. In consequence, the Gospel we have just heard presents us with two obvious questions: did this miracle happen, and, if it did, what does it signify?

Firstly, then, did it happen? The Gospel-books of St Luke and St Matthew, very different though they are in many ways, agree that Mary did not have intercourse with Joseph but remained a virgin throughout the conception of her Son. Acceptance of miraculous events of this kind is not in principle difficult for anyone who believes in God. If 'God' is our name for the almighty Creativity behind the world, why should he not on occasion act directly (instead of through secondary causes), in order to follow up his purposes for history? But over and above this general principle which in itself is perfectly satisfactory we need to know further why we ought to accept this *particular* alleged example of direct divine action.

As Catholic Christians we give credence to the Church's tradition on the point because we hold that tradition to be full of insight into the original revelation on which our religion is based. The Church herself emerged from the founding events of which the Annunciation is one. In her corporate memory, she recalls that this miracle happened. In such basic matters of Gospel truth, her memory is permanently jogged by the Holy Spirit, not least through the text of the Gospels.

I said there were two questions this Gospel text suggests. The second runs as follows: assuming this miracle *did* happen, then what does it signify? What is the almighty Creativity behind the world actually saying to us in this event?

The meaning of the miracle lies in the fact that the Incarnation of the Word of God was an *absolutely new beginning*. Something happened so different from all other events since time began that it is like a new beginning for the world. The Creator assumed the life of a creature. He entered his own creation so as to bring it back to himself from within, by giving us a new model for our activity — Jesus Christ his Son, and a new set of resources for our activity — the Holy Spirit, who proceeds from the Father through that same Son.

On this Solemnity we are invited to respond to this new beginning, which is offered to us every year at this time.

APRIL

5 April, St Vincent Ferrer

Vincent Ferrer was a Dominican saint who died in Brittany in 1419. His family on his father's side was of English origin (probably their name was 'Farrer'), but they had migrated for economic reasons to Spain where he was born, at Valencia, in 1350. In this period Spain had a flourishing Hebrew-speaking Jewish population, which was used by the monarchies of the Peninsula for a variety of administrative tasks. In the course of his studies, Vincent became an excellent Hebraist, and something of a rabbinic scholar. As a priest he would bring large numbers of Jews into the Church.

Then there was a crisis apparently brought on by stress and overwork. The moral problems of society were colossal in the wake of the Black Death, and the schism between rival popes didn't help in the Church. He recovered his health: owing, so he believed, to the intercession of St Dominic and St Francis of whom he had some kind of vision on his sick-bed. They told him to rise and preach whenever and wherever he was needed. Now the international phase of his career began on journeys through Italy, France, Switzerland, and Germany. He preached in the open air, before massed crowds, always after a High Mass, with music played on a portable pipe organ with singing clerks to produce the sounds of early polyphony. During these preaching visits, penitents were enrolled, catechists trained, and hospitals founded.

His message was divine judgment, imminent now, yet also, and by the same token, grace abounding offered now: free pardon, full reconciliation with God. That is why Vincent was identified with the Angel in Chapter 14 of the Apocalypse of St John: 'Flying in mid heaven, with an eternal Gospel to proclaim to those who dwell on earth, to every nation and tribe and tongue and people... "Fear God and give him glory for the hour of his judgment has come and worship him who made heaven and earth, the sea and the fountains of water".' Lacordaire says somewhere that the first condition of a great life is a great ambition. St Vincent was given one.

7 April, St John Baptist de la Salle

We keep today the memorial of the patron of school-teachers in the Church. Jean-Baptiste de la Salle was a canon of Rheims in the reign of Louis XIV, France's *grand époque*. He resigned his canonry and disposed of a considerable personal fortune so as to embark on a new life, living side by side with other young men like himself (he was 30 at the time) who felt a call to teach the sons of the poor. From this initiative there grew the Congregation called the 'Brothers of Christian Schools' which at one time in the twentieth century was the largest of all Catholic educational initiatives, represented in every sector of education, from primary schooling to University teaching. Even in his own day, Jean-Baptiste already ran teachers' training colleges in addition to his actual schools. Incidentally, one of the latter was opened at the request of James II of England, then in exile, for the children of Irish Jacobites who had followed the defeated king into an unknown future abroad. John Baptist de la Salle was a dedicated, indeed 'driven', man of many austerities, whose high vision of Christian holiness was taken from the Christocentric mysticism of the great French masters of spiritual theology in his century.

In our day the association of ideas that joins young boys to clerics and monastics has become fraught as a result of scandals: scandals that are far better publicized by the media (why, we ask ourselves?) than are the corresponding examples of human frailty in civil institutions. That is why we need to remind ourselves that saints have pioneered that connexion, and made heroic sacrifices for its sake.

11 April, St Stanislaus

St Stanislaus is, in effect, St Thomas of Canterbury's Polish equivalent or, rather, forerunner: he was martyred for challenging the local ruler in 1079, just forty years before Becket was born. Unlike Henry II of England, however, Boleslaus II of Poland was not pitched against his bishop for reasons of principle: differing policies, differing convictions, about the relation of Church and State. The prince with whom Stanislaus was called to deal was, in the eyes of the martyr's biographers, quite simply a moral monster. No faithful bishop could stand by silent while his king gave public exposure to lust and anger on such a scale. Justice and mercy, not rapacity and cruelty, are the hallmarks of Christian kings. So Stanislaus inflicted the worst penalty the Church could impose: the sort of excommunication which made the person what was called *vitandus* literally 'someone to be avoided' a category that continued into at least the early twentieth century. It meant: no Liturgy could be celebrated in his presence. It was when he walked into the cathedral of Cracow and found that suddenly the services stopped that the king discovered his humiliation. Going one better than Henry of England he dispatched the bishop, not by proxy and on a nod and a wink, but by his own hand.

St Stanislaus does not exercise the psychological fascination of St Thomas. His was not the tardy conversion of an ambitious courtier but the steady growth in all virtues of an exemplary priest. But as if by compensation, the cause for which he died lacks the controversial complexity of Becket's case. He knew gross personal iniquity when he saw it and like Gwendolene in *The Importance of Being Ernest* he was not afraid to call a spade a spade.

23 April, St George

The two things most people would say about George—he slew a dragon and is the patron saint of England—are, I'm afraid, both based on misunderstandings.

St George had been venerated for centuries by the Eastern church as one of the greatest of martyrs before ever people in the West associated him with fighting dragons. The most likely explanation for the dragon is that an early account of George's life refers to the persecuting emperor Diocletian as 'that dragon', and someone later thought it would be fun to describe George's defiance of the pagan ruler by means of an allegory—an allegory with a point, which is found not just in the rescue of an innocent girl from cruelty, but in George's departing words to the people. That was when he told them to honour the sanctuaries of the Church and to look after the poor.

Those imperatives—protect the innocent, churches, the poor— would become very relevant to the attempts of the mediaeval

Church in the West to christianise warfare through chivalry, the adoption of a set of rules for soldierly behaviour by Christian knights. St George was the patron not so much of England as of the host of England: that is, of the English army, whose soldiers wore the arms of St George, a red cross on a white ground. The patrons of England remained what they had been: our Lady and St Edward, who had displaced St Edmund after the Norman Conquest. Besides them was now a new figure, the saintly 'protector of the realm'. The qualities ascribed to George in the hagiographic tradition—courage, a sense for justice, respect for the Church and a 'preferential option for' the poor—are certainly qualities we would want our soldiers to have.

As citizens we are in the middle of a sporadic but important debate about the future form of the British State, one key aspect of which concerns the reconstruction of English identity. Inevitably, that will raise the question of spiritual continuity with the older English history, prior to the union with Scotland and thus, for the most part, prior to the Reformation. So today's feast provides some food for thought: not only about what martyrs may attest but also about the significance of the patrons whom the English took for their own.

25 April, St Mark

Few people in the early Church were better placed than St Mark to tell us about the origins of our faith. For myself, not belonging to the school of thought which holds that early ecclesiastical writers got everything wrong where the authorship of the New Testament is concerned, I am happy to accept the identification of the evangelist Mark with the John Mark whose mother lent her house in Jerusalem to the apostles as their meeting place. John Mark's name is a combination of Greekified Hebrew, 'Joannes', with Latin, 'Marcus', and a cosmopolitan polyglot family like that fits very well with what tradition tells us about the Second Gospel.

The Book of the Acts describes Mark as the co-worker of the two greatest apostles, Peter and Paul, and, as we heard in today's epistle, Peter refers to Mark as his collaborator and, more than that, his 'son', indicating a close, a very personal, connexion.

All of this makes sense if indeed Mark accompanied Peter to Rome as his interpreter and, as it were, Latin secretary, as well as resident catechist. That is a multi-tasking job which would have encouraged him to get into order his and Peter's materials on the beginnings of the Gospel.

The tradition about Mark as it has come down to us reports that, following the execution of Peter and Paul, Mark went to missionise in the greatest city of the Eastern Mediterranean, Alexandria. In Egypt today, the Coptic Church sees itself as built on the foundation of Mark's preaching and martyrdom, just as Rome sees itself as so built in the same way but in relation to Mark's spiritual father, Peter. The Coptic patriarch styles himself 'the successor of St Mark' just as the Roman pope is 'successor of St Peter'. And if the patriarch also calls himself 'the teacher of the whole world', that is mainly a reference to another of his predecessors, a saint we shall celebrate next week, Athanasius the Great, whose robust defence of the divinity of Christ sometimes seemed to stand alone among his contemporaries in the Christian world.

We can be sure that Athanasius had pondered the significance of St Mark's Gospel with its transcendent Jesus, always ahead of his disciples in the road, who nevertheless goes to his destiny through suffering and patience, thus revealing that the Old Testament God of steadfast love has in the personal being of Jesus come into the world.

29 April, St Catherine of Siena

One of the needs of the Church today is a revival of spiritual motherhood. Of course, the Church never ceases to be our Mother. She became our Mother when she bore us as her children in the font, giving us the new life of baptismal grace. No one, says the Church father Cyprian of Carthage, can have God for his Father who does not have the Church as his Mother. But in order to experience the Church as Mother, is it enough to point to the existence of fonts and baptisteries? Surely not. The Church cannot be experienced as holy Mother Church rather than an organization of moralizing leaders and critical pundits unless there are a few, or more than a few, holy mothers around.

Catherine of Siena was only thirty-three when she died but she had long been addressed as mother by the so-called 'beautiful brigade' of her followers and by many of those she had come into contact with in person or by letter.

She was a practical mother. When she saw things that were wrong in the lives of the *Caterinati* she set about remedying them: pleading, coaxing, threatening, using the language of common sense as well as the language of the heart. And when she saw something wrong in the Church she did the same.

She was also a passionate mother: ardently, boundlessly, passionate for God in a way that dominated her being and inspired her short live. She was passionate for what she called 'the honour of God and the salvation of souls', and these two causes were closely connected in her mind. 'Do not be satisfied with little things', she told one of her disciples, 'for God expects great ones'. She was passionate for the Church, for the 'Mystical Body of Holy Church', in the formula she made her own, passionate for its reform, by which she meant, above all, having holy bishops and priests who could communicate the faith and the sacraments at their true worth.

And if we ask what their true worth might be, the answer she gave is, 'Blood'. It was, of course, the blood of the immaculate Lamb. That seems to have been the last word she spoke on 29 April 1380 in the house on the Via Santa Chiara in Rome.

> Lord you summon me to yourself. I am coming to you, not by my own merits but solely through your mercy, which mercy I crave from you by virtue of your Blood.

Spiritual mothers don't come from just anywhere. Like Eve taken from Adam's rib-cage, they are made from the gaping wound in the side of Christ.

30 April, St Pius V

There are, or were, two things many people in England know or knew about Pius V. Or rather there was one thing they knew—to draw on a Scholastic distinction—*simpliciter*, 'simply speaking', and another thing they knew *quodammodo*, 'in a certain sense'.

What they knew *simpliciter* was that Pius V was the pope who excommunicated Elizabeth I. In the words of Pius's Bull, she was excommunicated for deposing and imprisoning Catholic bishops who refused to acknowledge her as 'supreme governor of the particular church'. Further, she had entrusted the episcopal office not only to laymen but also to schismatics. She had also re-introduced an Oath of Supremacy forbidding ecclesiastics to recognise anyone other than the queen as 'supreme governor in spiritual and ecclesiastical as well as temporal affairs' in England. And it was by her authority that heresies were being preached through the realm.

The thing people knew or know 'in a certain sense' is the reference to Pius V in Chesterton's exuberant but also mystical poem *Lepanto*, a poem about the throwing back of the Muslim threat to Western Europe. 'The Pope was in his chapel before day or battle broke./ Don John of Austria is hidden in the smoke…' and so on. I call that something people know *quodammodo* because while many English schoolboys have learned the poem by heart few, I think, have been aware of the name of the pope. It was in fact Pius V, who has been called the least political of the early modern popes, but who was obliged to be political in each of two situations: England, and the Turkish menace to the Adriatic, with more success in the second case than in the first.

He was a pope with the highest expectations of himself and others—so much so that in Rome itself people said he wanted to turn the city into a vast monastery. He made much use of the newly founded Jesuits, but told them they must recite the Liturgy of the Hours in choir like all other Religious, though they needn't sing it if they couldn't bear it. He was a great pope of the Liturgy, as the rite which bears his name attests. In his love of the Holy Eucharist he was the first pope to walk bare-headed carrying the monstrance on Corpus Christi (previously popes participating in the procession were carried on the *sedia* wearing the triple crown), and was often seen on those occasions to be weeping as he went along. In all the offices he was given—prior, bishop, cardinal, grand inquisitor and finally pope, he lived as a fervent Dominican in prayer, fasting and study. This was what made St Charles Borromeo vote for him at the conclave which elected him, even though he had been very rude about Borromeo's uncle, the easy-going Pius IV.

This does not necessarily mean that people will rise to the top in the Church if they are fervent. But it does mean the Church was right to canonize Charles Borromeo, whose feast we shall celebrate another day.

MAY

1 May, St Joseph the Worker

In an older England, the 1st of May was the first day of Spring greeted with maypole dancing, parading around with the heads of oxen garlanded in flowers, and the consumption of copious quantities of cider. Something like that still happens at Oxford, by Magdalen Bridge, after the choristers of the College have greeted the dawn with madrigals from Magdalen Tower.

Superimposed on this native festival, and on the face of it rather incongruously so, is the European 'May Day', essentially a contribution of secular Socialism, a celebration of the rights and, subsequently, the power of labour. If that has anything to do with nature, it can only be, I suppose, the question of the natural necessity of labour power, the inevitable coming of a workers' State. That May Day was best seen not in the Thames Valley but in Moscow's Red Square. Nowadays, presumably, you would have to go as far as Beijing.

From the late nineteenth century onwards, the Catholic Church made strenuous efforts to steal the thunder of the Socialists. Today's memorial, St Joseph the Worker, belongs with the creation of Catholic trade unions, the development of Church social teaching, and the construction of new church buildings and attached facilities in industrial ghettos. Much of this is now as far distant from us as are the happy peasants of Merrie England themselves.

And yet of course most of us have to work, or need to work. Respect for labour, we can say, is not necessarily in contradiction with the veneration of nature because human work is a taking up of the processes of nature and a furthering of them. Nature is herself always working. As the metaphysicians say, linking the noun 'nature', *natura*, to the verb for 'to be born', *nascor*, she is *natura naturans*, the nature that is always in labour to give birth. We human beings are an unusual aspect of that thanks to our creative work.

A distinctively Christian understanding of nature and work would link both of them to the divine Creator. In order to re-align his own cosmos, and especially man, with himself, the Creator entered that cosmic setting and laboured with his own hands. The priest-poet John Gray wrote:

> Mary is busy sewing. Jesus stands
> Beside St Joseph; working through the day
> He did not come into the world to play
> At being man, but worked hard with both his hands.
> Thus he who built the world now condescends
> To learn the joiner's trade and handle saws
> And chisels for his bread, who made the laws
> Which guide a million planets to their ends.

2 May, St Athanasius

We celebrate today the man to whom, more than any other, the Church owes, under God, her preservation of faith in the divinity of Christ. Athanasius, the fourth century archbishop of Alexandria, taught with crystal clarity that the Word who became flesh in Jesus Christ must be thought of as existing from all eternity since he is God in the same sense as the Father is God with this single qualification: that the Word is 'of' or 'from' the Father, who himself is the Source of the entire Godhead.

Is this just a piece of abstruse religious metaphysics? Why does it matter? Firstly, it can hardly be said to be a trivial question whether we are to worship Jesus Christ as God or not. But secondly, only if the redeeming and reconciling actions of Jesus are really and truly the acts of one who is God do they actually 'save' us. Only then do they secure our present and our future in a definitive way.

Someone who realized this here in England and whose life and even times were changed as a result was Blessed John Henry Newman. Newman's researches into the Arian crisis showed him that we cannot do without this doctrine if we are really to assent to the truth that in the Church we gain access to a new and divine life. Newman and his fellow Tractarians discovered that enduring, valid, real Christian life cannot even be hoped for without such doctrine. Without the orthodox doctrine of Christ and the Holy Trinity we cannot even state or envisage for ourselves what the new life of which the Gospel speaks may be. The Oxford Movement, and everything that came from it, turns on this.

It is a doctrinal renaissance needed as much now as then.

3 May, St Philip and St James

The feast of the apostles Philip and James, has travelled about a good deal in the calendars of the Church. For many centuries in the West this feast was kept on the 1st of May, but with the advent of atheistic Socialism and the need for the Church to challenge the moral claim of the latter to the allegiance of the workers, May Day was turned over to St Joseph the Worker instead. Philip and James were then bundled off to the 11th of May. But before they had time to get used to the idea Pope Paul VI uprooted them again and dropped them down where they are today.

This calendrical instability reflects the mutability of theories about who they actually were. Was St James the character whose mother stood with the mother of Jesus beside the Cross? Was he the cousin of the Lord later regarded as the first bishop of Jerusalem? Did he write the New Testament letter which carries the name of *an* 'apostle James'? Was St Philip the same Philip whose numerous daughters play a part in early Christian legend, or was that the Philip the Deacon of the Acts of the Apostles?

At one level these uncertainties are owed to the fact that the apostles didn't make the effort to record plainly their adventures or afflictions for later historians to exploit. They had, after all, more important things to do than write in advance as modern newspapers now encourage people to do (at least in draft form) their own obituary notices.

But at a deeper level, this silence has to do with the lesson of transparency which our Lord, in the Gospel according to St John, gave St Philip. 'He who sees me, sees the Father.' The Word incarnate wanted to be a window through which men could look on the Father. The apostles wanted to be open windows through which men could listen to Christ.

4 May, The English Martyrs

There are rather a lot of English Catholic martyrs from the period of the Reformation and for nearly a hundred and fifty years following. Leo XIII beatified sixty-one (including eighteen Carthusian monks) in 1885 and 1886. Pius XI beatified another one hundred and thirty-six in 1929. Paul VI canonized forty of these earlier *beati* in 1970. Finally, John Paul II raised to the altars eighty-five new *beati* in 1987.

The forty selected for canonisation by Paul VI were undoubtedly well-chosen. They include the especially brilliant, like the Jesuit apologist Edmund Campion; the famous, like St Philip Howard, one of Elizabeth I's principal courtiers; and the representative, like St Anne Line who devoted her widowhood to looking after persecuted priests and St Margaret Clitherow who organized schooling in secret for the Catholics of York. The rest we can align with the great crowd of witnesses of whom St John writes in the Apocalypse that no man can number them, those who have washed their robes and made them clean in the blood of the Lamb.

Whether canonized or simply beatified, put forward for special veneration or left rather in the shade, these martyrs, however, have a great deal in common. Victims of a State allied with Protestant zeal, they belonged to a Communion which, albeit after considerable hesitation, exacted a similar fate from Protestants of all walks of life under Queen Mary. Naturally enough, we think of their age as pitiless. But does not our own age lack conviction? The intransigence of the martyrs frightens us, but then we no longer debate religious truth with such seriousness. We pride ourselves on remembering virtues of Jesus that persecutors forget: his gentleness, call to the disciples to love their enemies, refusal to meet violence with violence. But Christ did not die because he was compassionate. He died because he witnessed too uncompromisingly to the truth of God. In remembering the virtues the persecutors forgot, do we neglect the virtues the martyrs remembered?

Certainly when I became a Catholic in 1966 'the martyrs' were a vital part of the religious culture I entered, partly because it was in Lancashire which had more than its fair share. 'The Blessed Martyrs of England and Wales' stood for the specific claims of the

Catholic Church to be the one true Church of Christ, a faith worth dying for and so worth living for: a Church which, far from being un-English, had made England, had fostered its culture and unity throughout the Anglo-Saxon and mediaeval periods. They were also symbols of militancy, at any rate following the Second Spring as proclaimed by Newman at Oscott in 1849: the Catholic revival, confident of ecclesial advance and of the eventual if delayed re-conversion of England.

This is not the place to analyse the setbacks which followed in the later twentieth century. But if we are serious about evangelization it is necessary to re-learn the prayer Hopkins wrote from the heart for the conversion of England in his 'The Wreck of the Deutschland'.

> Remember us in the roads, the heaven-haven of the reward;
> Our King back, Oh, upon English souls!
> Let him easter in us, be a dayspring to the dimness of us,
> Be a crimson-cresseted east,
> More brightening her, rare-dear Britain, as his reign rolls...

8 May, The Patronage of the Blessed Virgin Mary over the Order of Preachers

Today's commemoration of the patronage of Mary over the Order of Preachers invites us to think about the Dominicans and Mary. There are two things to note, I believe: intensity and specialness.

First, the intensity of the Marian dimension to the lives of the early Dominicans. We don't generally think of the Dominicans as a particularly Marian Order despite the Rosary having become for some centuries an obligatory part of the habit. Some of the better-known Marian Congregations in the modern Church are likely to strike us as where 'all that' is to be found. And yet it would be hard to exaggerate the Marianism of the first Dominicans.

The acts of St Dominic's canonization speak of his frequent reciting of Marian antiphons and hymns, and it seems to have been widely credited that the founding of the Order was owed to Mary's intercession. In *The Lives of the Brethren*, an anthology of early Dominican experience, a quarter of the stories concern brothers who entered the Order because they were convinced that the

Mother of God was asking them to, and, so they thought, they had kept faithful to its way of life thanks to her prayers. This was the first Order which included a promise of obedience to Mary in its profession formula, reflecting this general belief in her 'co-foundation' of the Order with St Dominic. The daily procession in her honour after Compline was and in some places still is the most lyrical moment in the Dominican day.

So much for intensity. What about specialness? What was special about the Dominican devotion to Mary? Its main doctrinal theme was a very obvious one, the divine Motherhood. The Order of Preachers was founded to preach the orthodox doctrine of the Incarnation, with all its implications, and unless Mary is the Mother of God there is no Incarnation. But there was also something more distinctive and subtle. It was connected with the Order's intellectual apostolate as a whole. And that is the theme of Mary as the 'seat of wisdom'.

The Dominican spirit hails Mary as the mother of incarnate Wisdom: she who enjoyed the fullest spiritual penetration of the mystery of her Son. As the childhood of Christ draws to its close, she is reported as 'pondering' his sayings and doings, thereby becoming a model for theological activity. Likewise, as the original Eastertide draws to a close, she is in the Upper Room praying for the descent of the Holy Spirit, and there becomes the contemplative mother at the heart of the praying Church—the mother of the apostolic fellowship, and so the mother of the apostolate itself. She is, theologically speaking, the wisest woman who ever was, and that is why we have to stay close to her.

10 May, St Antoninus

St Antoninus was born in Florence in 1389, and joined the Order at a troubled time in its history. Painfully aware of its general decline in fervour, a group of devout friars set about the controversial task of reforming it in the 1380s and '90s. But Dominican life, like *ex cathedra* pronouncements, proved largely irreformable. When in 1406 the moral leader of the reform, Blessed John Dominic, was made archbishop of Ragusa (now known as Dubrovnik), the scattered observant communities fell victim to the wrath of their more relaxed brethren. As a result the young Antoninus, who remained totally committed to the cause of the reform, had no organized studies (except for a short course in logic), and had to rely entirely on his own exertions for getting a theological education.

It proved a shining example of theological self-help. Antoninus' *Summa moralis* was the first comprehensive guide to moral theology ever written, and, unlike some of its successor treatises, didn't forget to mention the Holy Spirit. As a theologian, its author was invited by the pope to help out at the Council of Florence, summoned for the great cause of reuniting the Greek and Latin churches.

Antoninus was preoccupied by the needs of different conditions of people in Church and society. As founder of the priory of San Marco in Florence, he made its library the first public library in Europe. He created confraternities for instructing children in Christian doctrine, and for the relief of the poor and the victims of the plague. In 1446 he deservedly became archbishop of Florence and left his city richer in both art and charity.

Observantine reforms are often written off as the work of petty-minded zealots, but St Antoninus was a Christian version of the Renaissance *uomo universale* or all-round man. His was a humanism transformed by the grace of the Gospel, centred on the following of Jesus, openness to the Holy Spirit and adoration of the Father. This is the kind of apostle we want.

14 May, St Matthias

St Matthias is the only one of the apostles whose remains lie north of the Alps, at Trier on the Western edge of Germany. This was the terminus of quite a pilgrimage for his relics, from Jerusalem to Rome, organized by courtesy of St Helena, and then from Rome northwards at the behest of the Holy Roman emperors in the eleventh century. His tomb does not seem to have attracted a notable cultus, on the scale of Peter's at Rome or James the Great's at Compostella. Perhaps it was because the inventiveness of legend rather failed him, or again because at least in modern times it is difficult to imagine Germans in ecstasy, even if in the Middle Ages figures like St Gertrude or St Mechtild show matters were once different.

Perhaps too the fact that, unlike other apostles, he was not chosen personally by Christ has something to do with it. Matthias was not just, like St Paul, a Johnny-come-lately among the apostles. He was also, *un*like Paul, who enjoyed an out-of-sequence Resurrection appearance of Christ calling him to his task, an apostle who was chosen by lot—chosen, it is true, by the other apostles, but nonetheless chosen by a game of chance, and so a second class apostle or so it would seem.

In fact, tradition knows nothing of this distinction between first and second class. Very human though the thought is, St Matthias received the fullness of the priesthood of Jesus Christ in just as the same way as the rest of the Twelve did, and this was at Pentecost. Pentecost remains the archetype of episcopal consecration, for the episcopate is the continuance of the ministry of the apostles in the Church insofar as it can be inherited after the founding generation. The Holy Spirit descended on them to launch and sustain the mission and life of the Church in its totality. That was the case then, for the Twelve, including Matthias, and, where carrying on their mission is concerned, the case now, when a man is consecrated bishop.

Sacramentally speaking, the way a candidate for the episcopate is put forward for ordination is irrelevant. Some ways of choosing bishops have been found imprudent perhaps because they fostered excessive dependence on temporal rulers, or tended to create organized factions in the Church, or impeded communion with the Roman bishop, the Church's centre of unity. The Coptic Church continues to elect its presiding bishop by lot, and since he may be an ordinary monk this is a present-day example of a 'Matthian' way of putting someone forward for episcopal ordination.

Of course we would all like our bishop to be chosen with the perfect consent of all relevant parties who on sight recognize him to be outstanding simultaneously as pastor, theologian, mystic, and administrator. Fortunately, this is not a necessary condition of being a successor of the apostles any more than it was of being one of the apostles themselves. It was enough that St Matthias was there with the others ready to do his best when the Spirit came.

And that is why on his feast day the Church can celebrate him as one of her pillars, like all the rest.

24 May, *The Translation of St Dominic*

St Dominic gets two bites at the liturgical apple. He has his main festival in August. But he also gets a message in Spring-time since around this day in the year 1233 his relics were removed from the rather pokey tomb where they'd originally been deposited in a suburb of Bologna and carried with a good deal of pomp to where they lie today, in the patriarchal convent, San Domenico.

At one level, this procession, with a papal legate presiding, was a rather grandiose way of opening the proceedings for Dominic's canonization. But at another level, it gave expression to a desire to have his remains accessible since it was known that he was to be a great intercessor.

The French writer Georges Bernanos, in his life of St Dominic, claims that Dominic died bewildered by his own death. It came, after all, at a bad moment, when his Order was just getting going. Bernanos was writing at the end of the period when the Romantic Movement had glorified the death agony. Its writers and artists typically maintained that in the moment of our death we can lift up a mirror to our life and as it were exalt ourselves by gaining a semi-divine idea of what it had all been about. Bernanos rejected this notion. It was incompatible, he thought, with the condition of a creature who, by definition, never gets a God's eye view of life.

So he put Dominic forward as an example of how to die. What was exemplary was the sacrifice St Dominic made of his death which he offered up in incomprehension—bewilderment—to God. So much so that, blessed by God for this very reason, it bore fruit for his Order. In Bernanos' words: 'round the dying father, who has now emptied himself almost totally of his mystical blood, his truly divine charity, the Order is buzzing like innumerable bees'.

What Bernanos overlooked was a crucial factor. Dominic was one of those saints (Thérèse of Lisieux is another) who on their deathbeds had a premonition of a future heavenly ministry of intercession. They knew they would be great intercessors, great 'askers-for'. That is really what today's memorial celebrates.

25 May, St Bede

St Bede is the only native English doctor of the Church. He was born in 673 and educated at the Northumbrian monasteries of Wearmouth and Jarrow, the second of which he joined. He describes his life as given over to the study of Scripture, 'amid [as he puts it] the observance of monastic discipline and the daily charge of singing in church'. Yet like many early mediaeval people, he was fascinated by just about everything knowable: language and grammar, science and chronology as well as history and the lives of the saints.

Though he regarded his twenty five works of biblical commentary as the really important part of his output, most of those who know of him today do so because of his *Ecclesiastical History of the English People*. Along with his lives of the Northumbrian saints, it gives us a unique glimpse of what this country was like at the start of its recorded history, and how our religion was interwoven with the first stirrings of national self-awareness, as well as the development of ethos and culture beyond the stage of barbarians obsessed by war, gold-hoards and tribal loyalty.

In 1565 Thomas Stapleton, a Catholic in exile for the faith, translated Bede's history into English for the first time, and published it with a not very ecumenical letter-prefatory addressed to Elizabeth I. 'In this history it shall appear in what faith your noble Realme was christened…, your highness shall see in how many and weighty points the pretended reformers of the Church in your Grace's dominion have departed from the pattern of that sound and catholic faith planted first among Englishmen, … and described truly and sincerely by Venerable Bede so called in all Christendom for his passing virtue and rare learning, the author of this history…' It is unusual for an historian to be a doctor of the Church and yet our faith is inseparable from a history, a story, so perhaps it's not surprising that someone who was able to reconstruct our national origins as a narrative based on divine Providence should be called a 'candle of the Church'. That was what St Boniface called him when he heard how he had died dictating the last sentence of his version of St John's Gospel and singing the Ascensiontide antiphon on the 26th of May, 735.

26 May, St Philip Neri

The desert fathers abandoned culture for holiness; we today tend to abandon holiness for culture. But St Philip, born in Florence in 1515, triumphantly combined the two.

The inner heart of his life was ascetical and mystical, even eremitical. He lived as a hermit for two years and frequently spent entire nights praying in the catacombs — then recently re-discovered — or in the Roman churches. He went into ecstasy so often that the man who served his Mass would frequently disappear for an hour or two and return when Philip had come back to normal functioning. Those certainly seem signs of an unusually intense commitment to the quest for holiness. They were, however, reserved for night time or, in the case of the Mass, the very early morning.

During the daytime Philip's life-style was completely adapted to the Late Renaissance urban society of his own epoch. His apostolate started out in engaged conversations with bank clerks and shop assistants. Then he moved up the social scale. He re-animated the Christian lives of urban sophisticates through using the art of music to the full in the services and conferences he arranged, giving a name eventually to a new musical art-form, the 'oratorio'. He devised for them various ways in which rekindled charitable energies could be put to use in the service of the needy.

St Philip's personality was the reverse of solemn or pious. He is described as happy and considerate, and he played enough practical jokes to be placed by some in the Eastern Orthodox category of saint called the 'holy fools'. These proclivities did not discourage a stream of visitors who came to his room at the extravagantly conceived Chiesa Nuova he had built, in place of a dilapidated church given him by the pope. At the end of a long day of receiving people, on 25 May 1595, he said, 'Last of all, we must die', and did so.

27 May, St Augustine of Canterbury

In 596 an Italian monk, Augustine, was chosen by Pope Gregory I to head an evangelizing mission to the Anglo-Saxons. He came from a civilization already ancient and a church nearly half a millennium old. Naturally, he was a bit apprehensive as to what he might find among the barbarians on the wrong side of the English Channel. In France he almost turned back but his nerve was stiffened by letters from the pope.

Amazingly, all went well. Soon the king of Kent's capital, Canterbury, was a flourishing ecclesiastical centre, well provided with books, and things needed for a decent Liturgy, and a scriptorium where Augustine helped the king to draft the earliest Anglo-Saxon written laws. From this centre, missionaries radiated out in all directions, including to Londinium, an over-rated little place left behind by the retreating Romans.

Behind every successful executive there is always an inspired researcher. Augustine's backroom boy was the pope who had an accurate idea of what England was like based both on access to imperial records and inspired common sense about pagans emerging from barbarism. The pastoral methods Gregory proposed made history in terms of missionary strategy. I suppose St Gregory is the real apostle of the English but he would have got nowhere without the man of action—the monk of action, St Augustine.

Today, when the prospect of re-evangelising England looks daunting, we can take heart from their success, and not least from that very human wobble when Augustine got half-way here and suddenly felt that Teutons prancing round sacred trees in honour of Wodin was not his cup of tea. Or glass of Chianti.

31 May, The Visitation

Usually we think of our Lady, naturally enough, in connexion with God the Son who as man is the Fruit of her womb. This was the message to us of the feasts of the Annunciation and of Christmas. We also think of her in relation to God the Father, who chose her from all eternity. That will be the message of the feasts of the Immaculate Conception and the Nativity of Mary later in the year. But we sometimes forget her relation to the Holy Spirit who, however, the Gospel for the Annunciation describes as 'overshadowing' her, hovering over her with his transforming presence. It's (among other things) lest we neglect this aspect of her mystery that the Church gives us this feast of the Visitation.

In today's Gospel, it's when her cousin hears the greeting of Mary that Elizabeth is filled with the Holy Spirit. As Mary comes into contact with Elizabeth, the Spirit is passed on to her. Of course, the Holy Spirit is immediately related to each person to whom he comes. And yet he is genuinely passed on by one person to another in what we can call 'incarnate' ways. And in the later Church, whenever Mary is around, the Holy Spirit seems to be around as well. One way we celebrate, in the time after Pentecost, the Father's sending of the Spirit through the risen Christ is by honouring the effect of that sending in the person of Mary—that effect which is the person of our Lady as not only a woman who was Spirit-filled but a woman who was Spirit-*giving*.

Just before his death, Jesus tells the disciples that he will 'not leave them orphans'. He is not going to leave them comfortless, desolate. But Jesus could not be said to have kept that promise if Christians never received any real mothering. It is part of the evangelical experience that the Holy Spirit works to mother us, to save us from being desolate, and does so (we say as Catholics) precisely through Mary. The cult of Mary as Mother of the Church is, I believe, profoundly pneumatological. It is all to do with the Holy Spirit.

The Holy Spirit is described in St John's Gospel as the Paraclete, the gracious Advocate. In the *Salve Regina* we say the same of Mary: *advocata nostra*. The Spirit is the Comforter of the afflicted; according to her litany so is Mary, *consolatrix afflictorum*. The Spirit comes to our help, and Mary is the help of Christians, *auxilium christianorum*, the same litany tell us. We could perhaps even venture the speculation that our Lady is the image of the Holy Spirit just as Christ is the image of the Father. And above all, in the Liturgy we call to mind how her intercession (thanks to the Assumption when she joins her Son in glory) is a universal intercession which has expanded to the dimensions of the Spirit who prays in all in sighs too deep for words.

Saturday after the Second Sunday after Pentecost, The Immaculate Heart of Mary

For the language of the spirituals, which for once is the same as the language of the man in the street, the heart is the centre of the personality. The Second Vatican Council reminds us of the objectivity of this when the conciliar fathers say of our Lady, 'The Virgin Mary... received the Word of God *in her heart* and in her body'. That reception in her heart was never subsequently lost, neither in the sequence of her great sorrows, nor in the glorification of her bodily Assumption.

When we open ourselves to Mary's heart we are not indulging in sentimental subjectivity. We are opening ourselves to something that exists in a supernatural mode, and in that mode is objectively good and objectively active—active with a view to reforming our untrustworthy subjectivities, in fact. To cite the Council again, '[She is] not merely passively engaged by God but... freely co-operat[es] in the work of man's salvation'.

With Christ, she is the source of initiatives precisely because she is immaculate, a free channel for God's life. It is the non-immaculate, those whose hearts are clogged up by accumulated rubbish, who are spiritually sluggish, always needing to be roused. The immaculate are spiritually active, spiritually creative.

JUNE

1 June, St Justin Martyr

St Justin was born in Palestine about seventy years or so after the death of our Lord. He came from Nablus, one of the hot spots of the present-day Arab-Jewish confrontation. He wasn't, however, a Jew, and in the second century could hardly be called an Arab. He was a pagan by upbringing, and, although a professional philosopher, he chose to become a Christian. I said 'although'; he would have said 'because'. His contribution to the Church chiefly consists in presenting her faith as the true philosophy.

Justin held that human reason exists by participation in the Word of God, the Logos. Animals such as we are couldn't work out the truth unless they were given a share in a higher order of things. In every human being is a seed of the Logos which can come to life in the form of rationality.

But Justin was not simply a humanist who believed in God. He went further, as he had to do if he were to apply for Baptism. He was in fact a passionate convert to the Gospel, who wrote a sympathetic account of the Mass-rite with a view to getting imperial toleration for the Church. And he died as a martyr. So he went well beyond the philosophical starting-point. In his own words: 'Our doctrine goes beyond all human teaching because we have the Logos in his entirety in Christ, the Logos that has been manifested for us: body, reason and soul.' St Justin explains that Christ is not only as God the eternal law of reason and thus the criterion for how we should think and act. He is also as man the New Covenant: the new invitation to make life a personal partnership with God in the company of the rest of his people.

3 June, St Charles Lwanga and his companions

We remember today the proto-martyrs of Black Africa. Africa had already had its martyrs in the early Church, but this was Roman Africa, along the shore of the Mediterranean, in what are now the Arab countries north of the Sahara. The saints we celebrate today are the first martyrs of the sub-Saharan south. They are black saints, who lived in Uganda not far from the border with the Sudan whose name means, indeed, 'black'.

Charles Lwanga was the major-domo of the kabaka, or king, of Buganda. He was a Catholic convert, while the king, by contrast, practised one of the African religions now called 'traditional'. Charles incurred the kabaka's rage when he tried to dissuade the royal pages from co-operating with the king's degraded sexual habits, habits which would fall under the headings of sodomy and paedophilia. The infuriated ruler proceeded to decree death for all who practiced Christianity.

Given the option of conformity or death, seventeen young men and two soldiers preferred death, and death they underwent with exemplary courage and even cheerfulness. Those of noble birth were beheaded; commoners were wrapped in mats of reed and set alight.

Like all martyrs, the martyrs of Uganda (who also had Anglican counterparts) died for faith in Christ, but more especially they died for the ethical implications of such faith. They remind us of the holiness of the moral law and the seriousness of the moral life. As with all martyrs, their example helped to spread the faith and deepen its hold on minds and hearts.

4 June, St Peter Martyr

Yesterday the Roman Liturgy celebrated the Proto-martyrs of Black Africa. Today the Order of Preachers celebrates its own proto-martyr, St Peter of Verona. The Church attaches an understandable importance to proto-martyrs, because they show that some new movement or mission is evangelically serious. But proto-martyrs come in various shapes and sizes. To combine an acute sense of the moral law with life at a corrupt pagan African court might be thought to lead naturally to martyrdom. But how on earth did a thirteenth century friar get martyred in, of all places, Italy?

Mediaeval Italy contained not only Dante, St Francis and the marvels of the International Gothic but also a variety of weird if not wonderful heretical movements of which the most important was Catharism—the sect St Dominic had come up against half a century before in France. Now let us make no bones about it: Peter of Verona was an inquisitor. As such he naturally aroused opposition, and the death he died was the death an inquisitor might expect. Though he was an exemplary friar, devoted to observance, study and spiritual direction, it was as a martyr that his Order remembered him, calling him 'Peter Martyr', and requiring at an early General Chapter that his image be displayed in all Dominican churches. Typically, he is portrayed with an axe wound in the head, a dagger in the shoulder, and fingers to his lips.

That last feature may be a reference to contemplative silence or it may refer to his last gesture when dying when he wrote in silence the first words of the Creed on the ground beneath him in his blood. Though he could not speak, he died proclaiming the Creed.

Peter Martyr inspired a theology of the so-called 'triple crown': a saint who was a virgin, a doctor, and a martyr, even if he was only a doctor, a teacher of the faith, in a wide sense of that word. By englobing in himself all three titles, he became as a modern study of him has put it, 'the Dominican's ideal Dominican', to the point of overshadowing the founder himself.

In all three respects, he showed a costing commitment to that biblical truth which the Creed sums up. Without such commitment, the Church slips about on shifting stands. The Carthusians have a motto: 'Let the Cross stand as the world revolves'. We do not want the terms of that motto to be stood on their head.

5 June, St Boniface

St Boniface was born in Devon around the year 675 and given the name Wynfrith which quite understandably he changed to something else when he had the chance. He proved an exemplary monk with an excellent grasp of Latin which later would be demonstrated in letters to the pope. He was also courageous. He elected to leave England and become a missionary to the pagan Dutch and Germans.

His missionary activity covered large areas of the Teutonic world from the North Sea to Bavaria. It combined personal heroism with an imaginative and practical vision of how to get the Church established. This involved two things. First, Boniface followed up the initial missionary approach by founding monasteries of monks or nuns whose task it was to form a Christian civilization around them. He realized that a Church without a culture lacks nothing except a base.

Secondly, St Boniface didn't hesitate to use the goodwill of neighbouring Christian rulers to build up the life of the Church. Today it is hard to find a Christian government anywhere, but Boniface was free of the strange belief quite common nowadays that for the State to recognize the truth of the Gospel is rather wicked, or at any rate highly inappropriate.

On his feast day we commemorate more especially the personal heroism that brought him to a martyr's death just as he was preparing to confirm some new converts in the Dutch countryside. His body was brought back to Fulda, his main monastery in central Germany, which is still today the chief shrine of German Catholics and the permanent meeting place of the German Bishops Conference. It ought to give them more inspiration than is available to their English and Welsh counterparts who repair to an apartment behind Victoria Station.

'If you love me', says the risen Christ to St Peter, 'feed my sheep'. St Boniface was not a pope, he was a missionary bishop, but he understood that every bishop shares analogously in that commission given to the apostle.

6 June, St Norbert

St Norbert, the founder of the canons of Prémontré, the Premonstratensians, exercised a notable influence on St Dominic. The customs and observances of his Order, the White Canons, permeate the Primitive Constitutions of the Order of Preachers. Although we can't prove that Dominic was personally struck by the biography and overall ideal of Norbert, it seems likely: otherwise why should he have borrowed so much from the way of life of the Norbertine canonries?

Norbert was born around 1080 in the Rhineland into a high-ranking family connected with the Hohenstaufen emperors. Though a cleric (a secular canon) he led an opulent existence on the basis of his family's great wealth. In 1115 while out riding he had some kind of accident during a thunderstorm. The shock changed his life. He sold his estate and gave the proceeds to the poor, went to Rome, and confessed his rather scandalous life to the pope whom he asked for a suitably sizeable penance.

The pope's penance was unusual but also in keeping with the aims of the eleventh century movement of new evangelization we call the Gregorian Reform. He told Norbert to go away and preach the Gospel, which he did at first by becoming an itinerant preacher in northern France. But he didn't really want to preach save in the context of a community which could be a centre of sacramental worship and a school of wisdom—a very Catholic, as distinct from Protestant, view of preaching. In the valley of Prémontré, he brought together thirteen disciples who agreed to lead a life of exemplary austerity, but with preaching, the administration of the sacraments and pastoral assistance to the faithful at its heart.

In 1126 the pope agreed with some alacrity to approve their Order and at the same time made Norbert archbishop of Magdeburg, a position that enabled him to further the influence of his canons in reforming other groups of canons regular in France and Germany. Fifty years later St Dominic would join just such a reformed chapter of canons, across the Pyrenees, at the cathedral of Osma. The parallels between Norbert's idea and Dominic's are plain, though so also is the difference: namely, that in the Dominican case, the preaching of Catholic doctrine took clearer precedence over pastoral assistance which, generally speaking, was reduced to simply the hearing of confessions. I discovered in 1979 to 1980 when I lived in a Dominican priory of the Province of France, albeit in Norway, that the French Dominicans considered English Dominicans to be Premonstratensians in Dominican habits. When I gave a Retreat to Norbertines in their great modern abbey in Orange County, California, I also discovered that could be a signal compliment.

8 June, Blessed Diana and Blessed Cecilia

Today's memorial focuses on two contemplative nuns of the Order of Preachers in its first generation, one of whom is also the main source for what is known of the appearance and personality of the founder. They were Italian ladies, one Roman, the other from

Bologna. Committed to the ideal of a reformed monasticism, they saw in the early Dominicans, with their zeal for the faith and the practices of the spiritual life, a suitable male horse to which they could hitch their female cart.

In this period, before the rise of the exclusively female Religious Congregations of the Catholic Reformation, women had to make use of men for their own ecclesial purposes. This was all the easier in that St Dominic had had a go at setting up some monasteries for women before he founded the Order of Preachers. Historically, the Dominicans have rather blown hot and cold so far as their enclosed nuns are concerned. They were a valuable powerhouse of prayer, yet too many of them would overburden the Order and inhibit its mission.

That has never been a problem in England, where there was never more than a single monastery, even in the Middle Ages, with the exception of the years between the First World War and the 1960s when there were two.

More widely, we can say: insofar as the contemplative life is the most basic Christian life, a life content to be a disciple—a member of the Church with no further entanglements or enrichments added, this 'second' Order recalls the 'first' Order to a proper sense of priorities. God must come first even if everything else is in turmoil: this is the message of the Beatitudes. It is one that friars too can take to heart. Abbot Cuthbert Butler of Downside might have been addressing them when he wrote, 'A contemplative life is not a life where action is absent. It is a life where contemplation is present.'

9 June, St Ephrem

St Ephrem is a rather unusual doctor of the Church and merits our interest. To begin with, he spoke Syriac which is close to our Lord's own language, Aramaic. All the other Church doctors from the ancient world used Latin or Greek. Another unusual thing: he wasn't a priest. He was a simple deacon though he only escaped consecration as a bishop by the simple but effective device of pretending to be mad. But the really interesting thing about him was that nearly all his writing was poetry.

Ephrem took the whole of revelation and re-cast it into poetic imagery indebted to Scripture but going beyond it. You might think that would render doctrine vague and impressionistic. But at the hands of a great poet images can be high precision tools of expression. There is something especially appropriate about a theologian of the Incarnation, in particular, using this kind of vehicle, which appeals to the whole person, mind, imagination, feelings, in a way that corresponds to the nature of the Incarnation itself. The eternal Word in assuming our human nature took to himself all its powers, all its faculties, and expressed himself within them, so that our humanity could be in principle redeemed that is, healed and exalted in those very faculties.

So today we are grateful to St Ephrem whom tradition justly calls the Harp of the Holy Spirit.

11 June, St Barnabas

St Barnabas is one those rather shadowy figures in the New Testament who can lay claim to the title 'apostle' but not (unlike St Matthias) in the strict sense in which we give it to the Twelve (and to St Paul). That's reflected in the fact that in the Western Liturgy he gets only a memorial, not a full feast day. In the early Church, or so it seems, apostleship was 'participable'. You could share in it to a greater or lesser extent. There were degrees of it. In effect, it was by association with the original apostles that others could have a share in the apostolic commissioning to be the representatives of Jesus Christ in founding the Catholic Church.

Insofar as we know of it from the New Testament, Barnabas' career has two lessons for us. The first is a religiously based love of country, or to put it in terms at once more modern and more theological, the value of giving evangelical priority to the conversion of one's own culture. St Barnabas was a Cypriot, and he persuaded the apostles at Antioch to let him go with St Paul to preach the faith in that island. After his break-up with Paul, he returned there to complete the work. He realized that, generally speaking, we are more effective in our own culture since that is where our sympathy and understanding are keenest. That licenses the idea of home mission, which is the first lesson we can take from his life. Giving evangelical priority to one's own culture, one's own country.

But then secondly, as the Acts of the Apostles tells us, there was a disagreement between Paul and Barnabas over the refusal of their companion John Mark to missionise any deeper into the Asia Minor hinterland. It's impossible now to be sure how the dispute ran, but probably Barnabas and John Mark thought it more reasonable to concentrate on the sophisticated cities of the Mediterranean seaboard, cities that were potential diffusion points for the new religion. Paul, by contrast, had the idea of a symbolic preaching to the whole world by means of a series of extremely ambitious journeys which sometimes included pressing on into remote, wild and thinly inhabited areas, just for the sake of universal coverage. And that gives us a second lesson from Barnabas' life. We ourselves need to think carefully about both the practicalities and the symbolics of how and where and when to evangelise.

13 June, St Anthony of Padua

Anthony of Padua was one of the first generation of Franciscans, entering the Friars Minor six years before the death of St Francis. Apart from this, almost nothing about him is what it seems. Despite his title *Patavini*, 'of Padua', he was Portuguese. Invoked as the finder of lost objects, the only basis for this in his life was when a novice who had absconded with the saint's Psalter was scared into handing it back by a bad dream. Though he is a doctor of the Church he wasn't so much a theologian as a charismatic preacher, and even then much of what he has to say isn't so much about the doctrine of faith as it is about morals, a lot of it directed against economic vices like avarice and usury. The early Franciscans were largely, in fact, preachers of morals.

The least problematic part of the picture is the connexion of his cultus with the poor-box and the parish organizations for poor relief called 'St Anthony's Bread'. For it is true that Anthony had a great devotion to the poor.

Here at least, then, the sense of the faithful has correctly gauged Anthony's temper. And this might lead a Dominican to take a second look at that apparently rather subsidiary sort of preaching the Franciscans went in for, which some might call 'moralising'.

Ethics is sometimes regarded nowadays as just an appendix to Christian doctrine. But if we look to the teaching of our Lord, things appear rather different. The Sermon on the Mount shows the importance ethics had in the teaching of Jesus, and it is profound. In that Sermon, he speaks of his disciples as the light of the world, shining out through good deeds, and so turning others towards the Source of that light, the Father. The Good always sends its radiance: this is the fundamental perspective in which all ethics is possible.

But in the moral lives of disciples, so Jesus predicts, this radiance will have power to convert others to the Good and to initiate them into praise, the returning of glory to the Father. 'Seeing your good works, they will give glory to your Father in heaven.'

In the ethics of Anthony of Padua, what we have in word and deed is the testimony of a doctor of morals. The Church's teaching is not about faith alone. It is about faith and morals. More specifically, Anthony's ethics is focussed on the poor with whom the Good, when he took flesh, chose to identify himself. The Good came unto his own but his own that is, men and women as moral agents, did not receive him, except for those 'little ones', pushed to the periphery of the world, who were able to respond to him as their true centre.

And because human beings were brought into this world to reflect the Good, by finding it in the Poor Man of Nazareth they also discover each other. Once we live in and from the Good then the love of God grows through the love of neighbour, and vice versa.

And here we can find the deeper meaning of St Anthony's role as retriever of lost objects. He points the way to a revelation which recovers, for those who have lost it, what is most essential to their lives.

20 June, St Alban

We keep today the memorial of the only saint continuously venerated in this country since Roman times. If we can trust the traditions that have come down to us, he was a native of Verulamium, now St Alban's in Hertfordshire. During a local bout of persecution of Christians, Alban, who was still a pagan, gave shelter to a Christian priest who had sought refuge with him. He was sufficiently impressed to become a convert, and received Baptism. When soldiers came to arrest the priest, Alban exchanged clothes with him. Wrapped in his guest's long cloak he was conveyed to the magistrate who passed sentence.

Alban's crime was sheltering a sacrilegious person: a Christian presbyter who, set apart to represent the holiness of God in the midst of the *plebs sancta Dei*, God's holy people, by his very existence challenged the claim of the Roman State to be the mediator of the holy. Through re-locating the holy in the crucified Jesus Christ and the community founded by him, Alban's guest was a standing affront to the self-definition of Roman society.

Fourteen hundred years later, something similar would happen in Tudor England where a number of the English martyrs, such as St Margaret Clitherow, incurred the death penalty for, once again, sheltering priests who by their very existence denied the claim that the Church's holiness could be defined in terms of relation to the Crown.

In the modern period, the English Catholic Church mercifully escaped the anti-clericalism which marred the history of much of European Catholicism. The people recognized the priesthood as a sacramental reality which is there for them, to enable them to define themselves as a community vis-à-vis other communities competing for final allegiance, not through sacred claims so much as through secular ideologies of one kind or another.

Today we must be clear-sighted and recognize there is a tendency to minimise the significance of the priesthood, and even a threat to its identity. It would be tragic if in the name of a redistribution of functions in the Church, the Catholic laity came to define themselves over against the Catholic priesthood rather than using that priesthood to define the whole Church over against present or future parallels to the emperor Diocletian or Queen Elizabeth the First.

Tragic, and a betrayal of our proto-martyr, St Alban.

21 June, St Aloysius Gonzaga

Aloysius Gonzaga was a physically feeble child born in 1568 to a family of Renaissance courtiers who wanted him to follow in their footsteps. Like many chronic invalids he was determined that, on the contrary, no one would tell him what to do. In 1585, at the age of sixteen, he entered the Jesuits who were still in their first fervour. Careless of human respect, zealous in imitating the lives of the saints, especially in austerities and mortification, he further undermined his health. He contracted the plague while nursing the sick and died on 21 June 1591 when he was twenty-three.

Aloysius was beatified very quickly, only thirty years after his death: more swiftly than the Jesuit founder, St Ignatius, himself. The newly reformed Papacy reasoned along the lines: desperate times need desperate measures. Decadent milieux need uncompromising counter-examples.

The cult of St Aloysius raises a question. Is sanctity best seen in those who are culturally typical of their age (in the Renaissance, that meant, among other things, go-getting and adventurous), yet succeed in baptizing it, as with Ignatius? Or, as with Aloysius, is sanctity best seen in those who stand out against the least evangelical features of an age with peculiar heroism?

This in turn might lead us to ask, Is the Church's government more prudent when it builds non-confrontationally on whatever is good in contemporary culture, however limited that good may be? Or is it more prudent when it lays down clear lines of distinction, even battle lines, and says to people: 'Choose'?

There can be no unilateral answer to these questions, but the side to which we veer is revealing of how we see the relation between the Church and the world. According to doctrine, the Church is the only covenanted means of grace, the ensign to the nations. And yet the proverb is not without its wisdom that says, God writes straight with crooked lines.

22 June, St John Fisher and St Thomas More

The place is the Tower of London, the time any time between April 1534 and June 1535. In cells close by each other are the chancellor-for-life of the University of Cambridge, John Fisher, and the high steward of the University, its chief legal officer, who also happened to be high steward of the University of Oxford, Thomas More. They are the leading figures of Christian humanism in England. Fisher has transformed the syllabus at Cambridge and been a model bishop at Rochester. More has established an enviable reputation for probity as lord chancellor of England, keeper of the king's Great Seal. They are not allowed direct communication but they manage to smuggle to each other a few gifts. More sends Fisher apples and oranges and a holy picture. Pathetically, Fisher can send back only half a custard.

What has brought them to this pass? Every schoolchild knows, or used to know, that Henry VIII's desire to divorce his wife and marry Anne Boleyn triggered the events which led to the Act of Supremacy whereby Parliament declared the king Head of the Church in England and cut off the English Church from the pope, henceforth to be treated as a mere foreign prelate, 'the bishop of Rome'. Fisher and More were already in prison when the act was passed. They were there because they had refused to sign the earlier Oath of Succession which identified the offspring of Henry and Anne as heir to the throne. Their objection was not to the succession as such but to the terms in which it was couched which amounted to making the Oath of Succession an oath of acceptance of the King's supremacy in the Church.

As a canny London lawyer, More met the demand for an explanation by silence. Only the perjury of a Crown official secured his conviction. Fisher, simpler and more straightforward (he was a Yorkshireman), believed the courtier who told him that the King invited him to speak his mind frankly, with no question of penalization to come.

More, with his speculative intellect, foresaw in the collapse of the authority of his Church not only the disintegration of Christendom but the eventual unravelling of a humane civil order. Fisher, with his more practical bent, saw that collapse and disintegration focussed in advance on one issue, the question of marriage and therefore the question of society's most basic cell. In his speech at the judicial enquiry into the marriage he recalled how St John the Baptist had thought it impossible to die more gloriously than in the cause of marriage, and yet marriage then—in the time of the

Baptist—was not so holy as it had subsequently become, with the shedding of Christ's blood. Now it is a sacrament, a sign of Christ's own spousal love for the Church. Fisher concluded he must be adamant in its defence, whatever the cost might be. Fisher was a martyr not only, then, for the unity of the Church and notably for that bond of her unity which is the office of Peter. He was a martyr too for another sort of union altogether: the holiness of the union of man and wife. In a period like our own where heresies are above all moral heresies, this makes him very much a saint for our times.

23 June, St Etheldreda

St Etheldreda, otherwise known as Aethelthryth, Ediltrudis, or less jaw-breakingly, Audrey, was a major figure in the seventh century east of England. She began with notable advantages. Her father was king of East Anglia and he gave her the Isle of Ely as a wedding gift.

The wedding itself did not lead to ordinary married life. She was clear it would have to be a virginal marriage, something the Church had accepted following the precedent of the marriage of St Joseph and our Lady. Etheldreda made two of these arrangements. It was only when the Northumbrian king Egfrith, still in his 20s, pleaded with her to normalize their conjugal relations that she entered monastic life and in 673 founded the great double monastery of Ely on the territory of her dowry.

Though a ruling abbess, Etheldreda led a life of exemplary austerity, simplicity and attention to God. She died of the plague, probably still in her 30s, lamenting that the worst tumour, on her neck, reminded her of the ostentatious finery she had worn as a princess at her father's court. Her successor was her sister, who had been queen of Kent and was the foundress of Minster on the Isle of Thanet, which in the twentieth century was repopulated by Bene-dictine nuns from the abbey of Eichstätt in Bavaria. At her sister's instigation, Etheldreda's body was exhumed twenty years after her death, found to be incorrupt, and the tumour the sign, so she believed, of her human frailty fully healed. Her body was translated to Ely where it rested in a Roman sarcophagus, identified in the last century, though empty of its contents, at Grantchester.

Some of her much venerated relics found their way into Recusant hands at the Reformation. St Etheldreda's, Ely Place, in London, has an example as does the little Catholic parish church in Ely itself. An attempt by the canons of Ely Cathedral to recover that local relic through the instrumentality of Elizabeth II was frustrated thanks to the courageous obstinacy of the then parish priest.

I should like to see a church where great abbesses have wise counsel to offer bishops and laity.

24 June, Solemnity of the Nativity of St John the Baptist

This is a great feast, as I'm well aware from my time in Scandinavia, where St John the Baptist's day, and especially the night before it, is still a major popular festival, though it has long been paganised or, better, re-paganised, for it is a feast for the summer solstice with much junketing and carousing.

Of course this is not what the Church herself has in mind. In the *Confiteor*, the 'I confess', of the Mass of the older Roman rite, we don't (as in the Missal of Paul VI), call to mind only our Lady when naming particular saints whom we would wish to pray for us. We also implore the aid of St John the Baptist as well. True, we also add St Michael Archangel and the blessed apostles Peter and Paul, but even so this is clearly an exclusive list for ecclesial top people, meant to identify figures of outstanding importance, as distinct from an omnium-gatherum. And though St John the Baptist has been eclipsed by other saints in the West and even to a degree in the more conservative Christian East, the fact remains that in the revised Missal of modern times the Preface for this feast comes immediately after those of our Lady and the Angels, and so before that of St Joseph and those of all other categories of saint whatsoever. And more tellingly still, he is the only person, other than Christ himself and his Mother, of whom it is true that the Church keeps as a festival not only the day of their death but also the day of their birth.

When we compare notes with Eastern Catholics, especially those of the Byzantine rite, we find these indicators confirmed. Along with the Eastern Orthodox, they celebrate St John on the day after the Epiphany just as they celebrate our Lady on the day after Christmas. And they are not penny-pinching with their praise. Thus runs one of their antiphons for the Office of John the Baptist:

> O Preacher and Baptist of Christ, Angel, Apostle, Martyr, Prophet, Precursor, Luminary, intimate Friend, Seal of the Prophets, the most honourable of those who have been born, Herald of grace both the ancient and the new, enlightening Spokesman of the Word.

And in another text we read: 'We know that, in relation to the Lord, he is, after the Mother of God, the greatest of those born on earth.'

Over the icon-screen in most Byzantine Catholic and Eastern Orthodox churches there stands John, bowing in supplication to the glorious Christ, with the Mother of the Lord echoing his gesture on the other side. Though the Gospels never bring our Lady and the Baptist together, except at the scene of the Visitation when John is still unborn, still in Elizabeth's womb, the subsequent tradition of the Church closely unites them. In the words of another acclamation from the Byzantine rite, 'By a natural congeniality and by a common prayer, the two of you making only one: you, Mother of the King of all, and you, divine Precursor, pray for us.'

So what is going on and why all the fuss in the first place? We can begin by noting a general point. When the Word becomes man, he does not do so as an isolated individual. He at once enters into relations with a series of figures with our Lady, with St Peter, with the Beloved Disciple, and so forth, and these figures he allows, so to say, to *co-define* him, and in co-defining him to co-define too the pattern of our redemption. To wish for a Jesus Christ who was utterly abstracted from these relationships and stood alone without the Communion of Saints (as a certain kind of Protestantism seeks to so) is to want an abstract and therefore a non-existent Christ. When now we come more specifically to John the Baptist we shall see that he plays a very particular role within this constellation of figures around the Saviour.

What the Eastern Church has specially noticed is the way this role of John's parallels in a certain fashion the role of Mary. They are heroes of humility: a very distinctive humility because it's intended to let the claim of God in Jesus Christ stand forth. When

Mary is confronted with the news that she is to be the means of realizing the hope of Israel, the divine Motherhood that will make her the most blessed of all women, she responds by saying, 'I am the servant of the Lord: be it done to me according to your word'. We find the same with John the Baptist who says, 'He must increase, I must decrease'.

We call St John 'the Precursor', still quite a common term in English for a predecessor. But whereas we normally specify how someone was someone else's precursor or predecessor by saying it was in some function or in some respect, John is called 'Precursor' absolutely, without qualification of this kind. He is someone who has consecrated his whole life, his entire being, to the service of Another who comes after him. And the result is that all he has, all he is, takes its rise from this 'precursing'. There is a humility, a renunciation, that finds in such total service a secret joy. 'The friend of the Bridegroom', says John about himself, 'who stands and hears him rejoices greatly at the Bridegroom's voice; therefore my joy is now full'. That is a sacrifice of love, a self-renunciation that rejoices to let God in Jesus Christ have his way: his redeeming way, the way that will lead to beatitude, to true happiness, for the human race.

And what the Church holds is that this is not just an accident of John the Baptist's personal spiritual development. Right from the very beginning, when the plan of God for the salvation of humankind arose in the divine counsels, it was meant to be. Just as God made man was to have a human mother who was prepared from all eternity and especially from the beginning of Israel's history, and without that Mother the Word could not have entered the biological stock of the human race, so likewise God made man was to have a friend, a friend who was also prepared from all eternity and especially from the beginning of Israel's history, and without that friend the Word could not have entered the public space of society there to be publicly identified as who he really was, publicly recognized for it, publicly manifested as Messiah and Son of God at his Baptism in the Jordan, publicly attested by a preaching of repentance in preparation for his advent, his entrance on the social stage, as in his own person the very grace and truth sent by the Father.

That is why, in St Luke's Gospel, the birth of John the Baptist is put in strict parallel to the birth of Jesus himself. We can say to Christians who have no time for Mary, 'No Mother, no Son'. But we can also say to Christians who have no time for John the Baptist, 'No Friend, no Bridegroom', or, if you like, 'No Best Man, no Bridegroom'.

Each morning in the Office of Lauds we address the Baptist as this indispensable herald of salvation: 'As for you, little child, you shall be called a prophet of God the Most High, you shall go ahead of the Lord to prepare his ways before him, to make known to his people their salvation, through forgiveness of all their sins'. Now by the way of martyrdom that child has entered the life of the Kingdom and is with the Mother of God interceding before Christ's face.

28 June, St Irenaeus

St Irenaeus was a second century Father to whom under God we mainly owe the Church's escape from takeover by the most dangerous of the heretical movements of the age: Gnosticism.

The word 'Gnosticism' means a system about knowledge. Gnosticism was an elaborate speculation about the divine nature, and how that nature put forth various emanations—defective expressions—of itself, in the course of which it, or part of it, split up into fragments. For the Gnostics, those fragments now make up our souls or, rather, the souls of the more spiritually refined among us. Gnostics treated matter as irrelevant or worse to our salvation, which is essentially a question of becoming aware that we are really parts of the divinity.

In his response to the Gnostic errors, St Irenaeus put forward a vision as comprehensive as theirs but properly rooted in the biblical revelation. He described the work of redemption as what he called a 'recapitulation' of the creative action of God, aimed at bringing all things, matter included, to their completion. He took his cue from the Letter to the Ephesians where St Paul writes that in revelation God 'has let us know the mystery of his purpose, the hidden plan he so kindly made in Christ from the beginning, to act upon when the times had run their course to the end: that he would bring everything together under Christ as head'. That at any rate is how the Jerusalem Bible puts into English the Greek; in his version Mgr Ronald Knox is especially clear in his translation of the last verse: 'to give history its fulfillment by resuming everything in [Christ]'. That is a good summary of what Irenaeus meant by 'recapitulation'.

We are not, then—this was Irenaeus' key message—to sunder the Redeemer from the Creator. There is only one God, perfect and complete in his own being, and he is both the Creator of all things and at the same time the author of the redemptive process through which, in Christ, he intends the world to reach its goal in him.

The Gnostics aspired to be divine. This aspiration gave their mythology an element of genuine pathos. It is indeed our destiny that we should enjoy the vision of God. But this destiny is not to be seized for oneself (this had been Adam's fault, though Irenaeus treats Adam as an immature child, and children scarcely know better than to grab). No, the vision of God which is the life of man is the gift of God who 'is going to be seen', so Irenaeus writes, 'by those he wills, when he wills, and how he wills'.

28 June, St Peter and St Paul: the Vigil

The present Roman Missal contains a number of Masses for the Vigils of great feasts but with the exception of the Vigil of Easter these are rarely celebrated. They reflect the fact that for many hundreds of years preparation for feasts was almost as important as the feasts themselves. Until roughly the First World War, the day before every great feast was a fast day. In Ethiopia, incidentally, the week between Pentecost and Saints Peter and Paul is a week of serious fasting with only vegetarian food being taken. It is sufficiently widely observed for restaurants to remove fish and meat dishes from their menus.

The idea behind a Vigil is a simple one. It is rare for something that is unprepared to be fully appreciated. Of course, there can be marvellous surprises in life just as there can be disappointing anti-climaxes. But on the whole, the more eagerly we anticipate an event, the more we prepare for it, so the more, correspondingly, do we get out of it. It is on this simple principle of human psychology that the vigils are based.

Spreading a festival over two days, vigil plus celebration, teaches us something about how to inscribe the Christian religion in our biology through fasting and feasting. It also teaches us something about the use of time. It withdraws us that little bit more effectively from the secular use of time, by which I mean a use of time that is neutral in relation to God and his revelation. In a fast-moving society like our own, it slows us down in a way that helps our health: spiritual and even physical. It gives us time to imbibe the significance of the feast, to reflect on what it represents in terms of the whole Christian picture.

On the Vigil of Saints Peter and Paul the readings concern their conversion, while on the Feast itself they are about their office, their work. The reading from the Letter to the Galatians is a classic conversion account, and the only one from Paul's own pen. To call the Gospel text set for today Peter's commissioning as chief pastor an account of Peter's conversion is more unusual, and yet, I think, it is justified. Nothing that has happened so far in the Gospel story suggests that Peter 'loves' Jesus more than do the other apostles. Leaving aside Judas, we might say, quite the contrary. But when Jesus asks Peter if he, Peter, *does* love him more than the rest, Peter finds himself able to say, Yes. Sometimes, making a statement or a gesture creates in us for the first time the inner resources that go with the statement or the gesture. To say, 'I love you', or to make a gesture of reconciliation may be to discover for the first time that one loves somebody or wishes to be reconciled with them. And by balancing Paul's conversion with this Peter text, this is the claim the Liturgy is making.

As we know, without conversion, without the turning of the heart and mind to almighty God in his Son Jesus Christ through grace, there is no real faith, no real hope, and no real charity. Without conversion there is no true worship, no acceptance of vocation, no discipleship worth the name. Not just for Peter and Paul but for each of us, it has to begin here and re-begin here, day after day.

29 June, St Peter and St Paul

In celebrating Peter and Paul by a common solemnity, we are celebrating in fact the apostolicity of the Church—the rootedness of the Church in a commission to the apostles. And more especially, we're celebrating the apostolicity of the Roman church, the church (that is) of the city of Rome, which these two apostles confirmed in the faith by their preaching and the testimony of their martyrdoms. In the West, this is the only apostolically founded see there is, and so it's the channel of apostolicity to all the others.

In and of themselves, there'd be no particular reason to bring Peter and Paul together. Peter, virtually the first apostle to be chosen, was destined to be the guardian of the revelation Christ had brought and as protector of the apostolic deposit, then, the human foundation of the faith of the Church. Being converted, he will go on to 'confirm' in faith his brethren.

Paul is coming from somewhere else. He is the last apostle to be called, and, by his own admission, he was 'born' out of time that is, after the public series of Resurrection appearances had run their course. And his role is quite different from Peter's. He was the apostle of the pagans, someone divinely authorized to modify the received understanding of the Gospel so as to ease the entry of non-Jews into the Church. He is a radical or 'prophetic' figure, then, whose adventurous policies could only be justified, if at all, by their missionary fruits.

Peter the guardian, Paul the prophet: that's how it seems to be. These are simplifications, admittedly. We know from Paul's letters, for his example, of his great concern for the integrity of the Gospel tradition. The very term 'the deposit of faith' comes from his hand. But if the contrast is a simplification, it is not an altogether misleading one. The tension between Peter and Paul in the Book of the Acts of the Apostles shows that.

What brings together liturgically Peter and Paul and not, for instance, Peter and Andrew or Paul and Barnabas (couplings that, in general terms, would make more historical sense) is their role in the founding of the primatial see of the West which, according to Catholic Christians, is also the universally primatial see of the Christian world as a whole. Though we think of the Roman church and bishop mainly in Petrine terms and naturally enough, when matters like power and teaching authority in the community are at stake, for these are specifically Petrine concerns, still, the Roman church speaks of itself as both Petrine and Pauline. It regards itself as created by the preaching and witness of these two apostles *together*.

The Petrine factor in the apostolicity of the Roman church has to do with conservation. It's a matter of holding onto what Christ taught, and how the apostles understood what he did and what he was—all on the presupposition, of course, that Christ is God incarnate and that his coming, therefore, represents *the* moment of supreme illumination of human experience. Peter gathers the Church around himself in identity of faith, just as people of all nationalities go on pilgrimage to Rome which in that way is an image of the New Jerusalem of the end of time.

By contrast, the Pauline factor in Rome's apostolicity is about mission: about outward expansion and necessary adaptation. It's a matter of maintaining the momentum of the impulse given by the Spirit at Pentecost, which caused the apostles to speak in a variety of tongues and drove the Church onto the highways and byways of the contemporary world. And *that* is all on the presupposition that the Spirit really is Christ's Spirit, the Spirit of the Son, and so is the release of the free energy of God into the world. Paul sends out the Church on mission: adapting its message to the styles of different cultures, just as Rome has been, in Christian history, an ever-renewed source of missionary impulse.

The Church has to be both guardian and prophet. And popes are sometimes called to fulfil that double role in a spectacular way. On this feast the grace offered may touch us with a little of that combination ourselves.

3 July, St Thomas

It all seems very unfair getting landed with the nickname 'Doubting Thomas' for just one isolated episode at the end of St John's Gospel. Ah, but if you read the Gospel according to St John from cover to cover, you will find that it wasn't isolated at all. Thomas does the same kind of thing in Chapter 11, doubting Jesus' ability to overcome death, and again in Chapter 14, doubting where Jesus himself, after death, would go. And the habit is getting dangerous. In today's Gospel, Thomas is introduced as 'one of the Twelve' which may sound on the face of it a pretty neutral expression but is in fact a somewhat ominous phrase: in the Fourth Gospel it has been used previously only for Judas. There is something distancing about the phrase 'one of the Twelve', which mirrors the distance Thomas himself has taken up vis-à-vis the divine plan and its reflection in his Master's mind and heart.

Thomas wants proof and by his mercy to this doubter Jesus offers it to him. Thomas sets up a triple demand: 'unless I see'; 'unless I put my finger'; 'unless I put my hand'. And Jesus now comes and responds in a similar threefold way: 'Bring your finger here and see'; 'bring your hand and put'; 'do not be unbelieving but...' 'But what?', we might ask. Surely, 'Have faith': have the *contact* of faith. While not devaluing the importance of physical contact, contact within ordinary human limitations, the texts never says that Thomas *did* actually put his hand into the Lord's side. Close physical contact was in prospect: 'bring your finger', 'bring your hand'. But in the event it was transformed into the contact of faith.

We know something of what that means from the icons and sacraments of the Church.

8 July, Blessed Adrian Fortescue

Today's martyr is a good patron for those of us who tend to go along with the flow of life as the course of least resistance: those who don't work out, at least at first, the principles involved but just about see the truth dawning shortly before it is too late.

Adrian Fortescue was an Oxfordshire landowner with royal connexions through descent and marriage. He also had links with the Oxford Dominicans and probably those in London too (hence his presence in the English Dominican calendar). He was a pious man. What historians know of his religious attitudes is largely based on the comments he wrote in his copy of the Breviary, the Book of Hours, and in his Missal.

He appears to have accepted Henry VIII's Reformation until as late as 1538: four years after the break with Rome. He went along with the flow. Thus the government had declared that the word 'pope' was no longer to be used in England, but was to be replaced by the phrase 'the bishop of Rome'. Dutifully, Adrian deleted the word *papa*, 'pope', wherever it occurred in his prayer books, for example next to the names of canonized popes in the calendar, or in the Canon of the Mass and the Good Friday Liturgy. This was in accordance with a royal proclamation from the summer of 1535. He also copied into his Book of Hours the bidding prayers issued on Henry's authority in 1536 which reflected the king's adoption, with parliamentary approval, of the title 'supreme head immediately under God' of the Church in England. When in 1538 the government announced that the three feasts of St Thomas of Canterbury were to be removed from the calendar, Adrian struck through with a pen the relevant texts in his books.

But then towards the end of 1538 or in early 1539 Adrian Fortescue had a change of heart. We know that because he subsequently went back to the bidding prayers in his Breviary and crossed out Henry's titles: not only the royal supremacy over the Church but also, it would seem, the very words 'the king's most excellent majestie'. This, if discovered, was a treasonable act, requiring the death penalty unless clemency were shown.

Why? What explains the change? Lots of people know that in 1570 Pope Pius V excommunicated Elizabeth I and released her subjects from their obedience, but fewer are aware that in 1538 Paul III excommunicated Henry VIII and declare him deposed, after the assault on Becket's shrine at Canterbury. So far Adrian had gone along with everything, while not necessarily liking it: he even raised troops to fight the Northern rebels against Henry's religious changes, the supporters of the Pilgrimage of Grace. But suddenly the scales dropped from his eyes, and in the words of the Bill of Attainder against him presented to the House of Lords by Thomas Cromwell, the destroyer of the monasteries, in May 1539 he 'most traitorously refused his duty of allegiance which he ought to bear unto your highness': that is, of course, the king. He was executed in the Tower of London two months later, on the 9th of July.

9 July, St John of Cologne and his companions

Today's martyrs died in the sandy flatlands and islands of southern Holland, below Rotterdam, where the river Meuse (by this point in its journey speaking Dutch and called the Maas) joins its waters to the North Sea. They were put to death, so an older Catholic hagiography tells us, by Calvinist sea-pirates. That is perhaps too Habsburg-centred a view. The sea-pirates were ultimately successful local rebels against the Spanish Crown which governed the Netherlands as a whole. As a jingle from the English Civil War has it:

> Treason doth never prosper.
> What's the reason?
> Why, if it doth prosper,
> none dare call it treason.

John Haar or Heer was a Dominican from Cologne who heard of the travails of his co-religionists on the coast and volunteered to join them. He did so not from zeal for the Habsburg cause but from fervour for the Catholic faith. The especial animus of the rebels was reserved for the Blessed Sacrament and the connexion with the pope. The white Host, the sacramental presence of Christ, and the priest dressed in white who was his vicar in earth (the pope in question was St Pius V, who is said to have begun the convention of the white robes at Rome): the nineteenth century Catholic Revival was not perhaps entirely wrong in linking the two as identifying signs of where the Church of Christ is to be found in the world. What they have in common is the scandal of the claim to make Jesus Christ ongoingly present, tangibly in the Host, audibly in the pope, on earth.

Theologians will want to nuance these claims in certain respects, and, of course, to set them more fully within the wider corpus of Christian thinking. Yet in a supernatural perspective they are always going to stand out, to stick out, even to shriek out. The Host and the pope are stumbling-blocks for those who for whatever reason—which could be anything from Calvinism to Humanism—cannot accept the claim that Jesus Christ is still materially available (the Host) or kerygmatically active (the pope) in such specifiably particular ways in the Church.

St John and his companions are shown in art hanging in their religious habits from the rafters of a Dutch barn, with a thrown down Eucharistic monstrance beneath their feet. They take their place in the long line of martyrs who have died for the incarnational materialism by which the Word entered the world and wants to be found there now in all the media of his Incarnation: in his sacred humanity, in the Blessed Sacrament and the other sacraments, in the *cultus* of the Mother of God, in the apostolic ministry around Peter, in the icons of the Saviour and those of his Mother and the saints.

11 July, St Benedict

Benedict of Nursia was in one sense a typical member of the Roman patrician caste of the sixth century. Faced with the breakdown of government, education and even agriculture this cadre of people used the Church, to which many of their families had been converted, to restore the fabric of a civilization. A Benedictine monastery, as originally conceived, is an elective version of a Roman seigneurial estate, with the abbot occupying the position of *paterfamilias*, ruling with the famed Roman qualities of sobriety, moderation, and a spirit of justice those placed under his care.

For the Rule of St Benedict itself, however, the monastery is not, as it appears to the social historian, an ecclesial version of a social form of its day. It is a school of the Lord's service, where the abbot is a Christophany, a manifestation of Christ whose qualities, as described in the Gospels, he must marry with those of an equitable governor. In other words, the social form has been rendered open to God in Christ and made capable not just of Christianisation but of 'Christification': of being a vehicle of Christ's grace.

All this is made possible by the radically theocentric quality of the life which the Rule offers, a life where all is to be turned to the God disclosed in Scripture as to its true centre. The sign of this is the *Opus Dei*, the Liturgy, to which, so Benedict insists, nothing is to be preferred. As the Second Vatican Council would put it, the Liturgy is 'the source and culmination' of the Christian life. Here Christ's Bride prays with and through her Head; Jesus Christ shares his heavenly intercession with his members, his Body; the distance which separates creature from Creator and sinner from the Sinless One is annulled, and man enters by anticipation his true home, to which all experience of society here is but the prelude and the preparation.

There is a vast contrast between ordinary life now and the life that will be in meta-history, in the Age to Come. But then there is also a big contrast between what Benedict did and what came out of his work even in historical time. In his own lifetime St Benedict was a virtually unknown figure who pottered about central Italy founding monastic centres for the local peasantry. Fifteen hundred years later he was declared the patron of Europe. In between these two dates, lies a millennium and a half of Benedictine activity in agriculture, craftsmanship, education and scholarship which changed the face of early mediaeval Europe from Spain to Hungary.

Pope Paul VI declared Benedict patron of Europe not because he was a monastic founder but because the movement he initiated was the most successful instrument of the Christianisation of culture the Church has known, and because (as the pope realized) the pastoral work of individuals today and tomorrow will be utterly evanescent in the wider society without a creative transformation of the culture in which we live, analogous to that of the Benedictine centuries.

As we look around Europe now and ask where that is happening the answer can only be: in small pockets. On the wider scene, the Church is largely impotent as a cultural force.

Yet we can take some comfort from St Benedict's obscurity in his own lifetime. Having sown the seed, the Holy Spirit watered and gave the growth in his own good time. Perhaps the Rule of St Benedict with its masterly combination of strict principle and *humanitas*: not just the Roman virtue but what the Bible calls the goodness and humanity of God our Saviour, provides us with the clue we need.

15 July, St Bonaventure

St Bonaventure was a Franciscan contemporary of St Thomas, living, then, in the middle decades of the thirteenth century. He became the head of his Order, its minister-general, and a cardinal. But we are remembering him today as a holy doctor: a saint and doctor of the Church.

Is it possible to put his teaching in a nutshell? The centre of it is Christ to a degree unusual even for theologians, and this alone would be a sufficient reason for honouring him. We must never be put off by accusations of pietism or devotionalism from giving our Lord the central place in our religion. It is in Jesus Christ, by way of his human form, that we shall, please God, one day enjoy the vision of God, and in the words shared by the 'Penny Catechism' with Hollywood, be happy for ever afterwards.

For Bonaventure, Christ is the centre both of nature and of history. Nature is the book of creatures in which, once enlightened by Scripture, we can read of him, the creative Word. History is the medium by which the world enters into the Kingdom of Christ, there to be presented by him to his Father.

We bring the two together at the altar, in the Eucharistic Liturgy, where we offer God the praise of the cosmos and plead for the world, asking that its history may bring it to its ultimate destiny in him.

16 July, Our Lady of Mount Carmel

Carmel is a high hill or, if you prefer, low mountain, on the coast of Palestine. It was associated with the prophet Elijah. The presence of his cave there attracted Christian monks once the ascetic movement had got underway in the early Church. Elijah was, after all, a contemplative who heard the still small voice of God. An even greater model of contemplatives, though, was the Blessed Virgin Mary, who received the Father's Beloved into herself and gave him flesh, later pondering his every deed in her heart.

In the Crusading period, hermits who were Elijah-inspired and Mary-inclined, and belonged to the Latin rite, were transported to the West out of harm's way during the 'Middle East Conflict' of that period. In 1226 at a general assembly here in England, they adopted a new rule allowing for the common life and an active apostolate: a decision seemingly confirmed by an appearance of the Mother of God to their leader, St Simon Stock. Today's feast was instituted to celebrate this event and, more particularly, the giving of the 'brown scapular' with the promise that those who wear this symbolic piece of the material of the Carmelite habit will enjoy Mary's unfailing protection until death.

That is a piece of poetry, not literal theological prose, and we should interpret it accordingly. How shall we do so? As was proclaimed at the end of the Second Vatican Council, Mary is the Mother of the Church. Her compassionate intercession for the adopted brothers and sisters of her Son is like a cloak thrown around the shoulders of cold and exposed travellers in this life. Mary cannot literally save, but she can be used by God to assist the working out of salvation in human lives, as pilgrims approach their goal, the 'mountain' that is Christ.

22 July, St Mary Magdalen

Mary Magdalen has often been regarded as the first preacher or preacheress of the Gospel. As we have just heard in the Liturgy of the Word, she it was who took the message of the Resurrection to the apostles. So behind the all-male apostolic ministry there is a woman who by the closeness of her relation with Jesus made that ministry possible.

St John's account subtly underscores the difficulty of recognizing the risen Christ. He is different, he has been transformed. Recognition is long drawn out, and finally comes when he speaks Mary's name, presumably with a characteristic inflection or pronunciation. In the Fourth Gospel he has already told his hearers that 'The Good Shepherd calls his sheep by their name and they know his voice'. She replies, 'Rabboni', which might be translated, 'My dear Master'. Her loving discipleship penetrates to his identity, and finds the rabbi of Nazareth in the glorious risen Son.

Generalising, then: it is the contemplative gifts of Mary Magdalen that qualify her to be the 'apostle of the apostles'. Though she lacks the public mandate to preach the Gospel, for which the apostles alone are commissioned, she provides something more. She provides those who are thus commissioned with their renewed relation with Christ.

There is a clue here for the sometimes disputed question of the inter-relation of men and women in the Church.

23 July, St Birgitta

St Birgitta, as the *Catholic Encyclopaedia* suggests, is the most celebrated saint of the Northern Kingdoms, and it was in part, no doubt, to bring into consciousness what for Catholicism sometimes seems the forgotten region of Europe, Scandinavia, that Pope John Paul II declared her a co-patron of Europe in 1999. She was also, in her own right, a remarkable woman.

Born around 1303 into a family of Swedish landowners, she first appears as a typical aristocratic wife: in charge of estates and caring for a large family and household. She must have achieved a certain reputation in these pursuits because in 1335 she was summoned to court to be a lady-in-waiting to the Swedish queen. She retained these connexions as the moral reformer, religious foundress and mystic she later became.

A pilgrimage undertaken with her husband, Ulf, led both partners to exchange their married life for a quasi-monastic life-style, and when Ulf died in the mid 1340s Birgitta received what is known as her 'calling vision' which gave her the vocation to be in her own words the 'bride and mouthpiece' of Christ. She spread the message of her auditions and visions by word of mouth, travelling through Sweden and further afield on what would now be called, I suppose, speaking tours. Her confessors also recorded their content in Latin, and these texts would later be published under the title 'Revelations'. The Swedish royal family supported her mission. The king, Magnus Eriksson, gave her the estate at Vadstena which was to become the site of the first Birgettine ('Bridgettine') monastery.

She meant her monasteries to be mini-models of the Church: the 'Order of the Saviour', as she called them. They were for both monks and nuns living in distinct but connected buildings, and under the rule of an abbess who represented the Mother of God. There were to be in each foundation thirteen priests, representing the twelve apostles plus St Paul, and four deacons to represent the four doctors of the Latin church. The total number of male and female monastics was to equal the sum of the original apostles plus the Lord's seventy-two first disciples: hence eighty-four. This concept, though not enormously practical, at least shows Birgitta's lively ecclesial imagination.

Her *Revelations* take as their theme the extent to which the love of God was willing to go to save us, as well as the need for conversion and fidelity since the mercy of God is not in contradiction with his justice. They probably inspired Julian of Norwich's *Showings of Divine Love*, just as Birgitta's activity as a Church reformer, notably after she took up residence in Rome in 1350, was almost certainly the inspiration for the public life of Catherine of Siena. Both Birgitta and Catherine worked hard to bring back the popes from Avignon to Rome.

These three holy women Birgitta, Julian, Catherine were, then, interlinked. Cardinal Adam Easton, a Norfolk man who was a monk of the cathedral priory in Norwich, knew all three, and when he wrote his 'Defence of St Birgitta' to vindicate the value of her *Revelations* and the example of her life he was tacitly defending all three figures, since the principal topic of his thesis was the ability of women in the Church to teach men. Any man—by which I mean 'male human being'—who makes a serious effort to investigate the works this trio left behind will, I hazard, have little doubt on that score.

25 July, St James the Great

In what single place could you have met St Francis of Assisi, St Dominic, St Louis of France, and the Empress Matilda, otherwise

Queen of England? Only one is known, Santiago de Compostella, the Spanish shrine of the apostle St James the Great whose feast we keep today. His shrine was by far the greatest place of pilgrimage Europe knew until the apparitions at Lourdes in the mid-nineteenth century and the popularization of travel to Rome for, above all, a glimpse of Peter's successor, at about the same time. In connexion with Compostella, kings issued general safe conducts for foreigners, and certain routes were given special protection. At one Pyrenean crossing-point, pilgrims typically consumed twenty thousand meals per year, and at one town en route there were guesthouses sufficient to accommodate twenty thousand pilgrims at a time.

What did these droves of people take off for on such a perilous journey granted the limited policing possible to any mediaeval administration and the primitive nature of transport? Not to see the Romanesque cathedral, or the grandiose episcopal palace, the magnificent library or even the statue of the saint covered in gold-and silver-leaf.

They went to be in the presence of the relics of the Galilean fisherman who had accompanied the Lord Jesus in his ministry, had witnessed the glory of the Transfiguration and the bloody sweat of Gethsemane. They reckoned that, where the martyred apostle's mortal remains lay, there his intercessory activity would be at its most intense. And who is to say they were wrong about that? The body and the soul never become wholly irrelevant to each other, even in death.

Were they the actual relics? Possibly they were. At any rate they stood in for them.

The cult of relics which should really be called devotion to the Communion of Saints is not greatly favoured in the contemporary Church, at least in the Anglo-Saxon world. Perhaps there is something the matter with our anthropology. And perhaps the result is that the saints withdraw more from our consciousness, which can hardly be a good thing.

26 July, St Joachim and St Anne

In the tenth century, St Peter Damian warns against inquiring about those things the Evangelists thought it inadvisable to relate, and especially about the parents of the Blessed Virgin Mary.

On the other hand: the apocryphal literature which tells us about Joachim and Anne is relatively early: it comes from the Jewish-Christian world where the early Church first took form, in a culture where memory played as big a role as manuscripts. And something must have given it credibility in contemporary eyes to start its circulation moving. Why should we not suppose that it contains at least occasional nuggets of historical truth—a truth which is also the inspiration for beauty.

In saying so I have in mind the Byzantine icons of Joachim and Anne which show them coming together before the birth of our Lady. On at any rate one interpretation of the iconography concerned, this would be the only portrayal in liturgical art of the marriage act, itself suggested with the utmost discretion in the flowing movements of their robes: a world away from the debased or trivialised images rampant today. These are the images known to the West as the *osculum Joachim*, the 'kiss of Joachim', and in the East as the 'Meeting of Joachim and Anne'. They are also the earliest images of the Immaculate Conception we know.

Something can be gleaned from the names of these figures. 'Anne' means 'grace'; 'Joachim' means 'the Lord prepares'. Our Lady was conceived by her parents—that of course goes without saying except to those who confuse Immaculate Conception with Virginal Conception. Biologically speaking, Mary was conceived exactly as we are. But there is more to be said, nonetheless. She was conceived and nurtured in a context where God was at work: both interiorly, in minds and hearts, and exteriorly, through the spiritual purification of the Jewish environment. Grace was given, the Lord prepared. That is how God always works on human beings, at once within and without, both by sanctifying grace, which changes us deep inside us, and by his Providence, by the things that happen to us.

Grace was given, the Lord prepared, and so the one capable of mothering Emmanuel appeared on the human scene, on the

Israelite scene. It is the woman we invoke in her Litany as the Ark of the Covenant and the Tower of David, the concentration of the promises to Israel.

27 July, Blessed Robert Nutter

Just two Dominicans are recognized as martyrs of the English Reformation, and both of them had only a tenuous relation to the Order. One, Adrian Fortescue, was a knight of the shire who before Henry VIII's break with Rome had bought letters of confraternity with the Oxford Blackfriars, making him a lay associate of the Order. The other was a secular priest who made profession by post during his fourth term of imprisonment for the faith under Elizabeth I. It was common for secular priests awaiting execution to become Jesuits, thus identifying themselves with the zeal of the newly founded Society, the spearhead of the Counter-Reformation, but Blessed Robert is the only example of one becoming a Dominican. At the time he was, so far as is known, the only Dominican in England.

We can only speculate as to why this typical seminary priest, born in a village on Pendle Hill near Clitheroe, educated at Blackburn Grammar School, trained for the priesthood in the English College at Rheims, took this unusual step. One suggestion is that it was out of an historical sense of what the Order of Preachers had meant in England. Wisbech Prison, where he made his decision, has been called the 'tomb of the pre-Reformation Church'. Everybody who was anybody and had survived was there: the last abbot of Westminster, the last Catholic bishop of Lincoln, Catherine of Aragon's last chaplain, and so on.

We might also ask why the challenge to respond to State-imposed heresy and schism found so little heroic response among the established Dominicans of the Tudor period. Perhaps they grasped at the straw that, under Henry, the national episcopate, with one exception, had sanctioned the breach with Rome, and thus had exercised a collegial authority to that effect. Whatever the reason, the English Dominicans did not value their Christian liberty and orthodoxy to the uttermost.

And so, to adapt St Paul, God raised up what was low in the eyes of the Order, mere nothings: a simple associate and a Johnny-come-lately, to put to shame that which was well-established and, no doubt, considered itself wise.

29 July, St Martha

It's often said of the episode of Christ in the house of Martha and Mary, as found in St Luke's Gospel, that only a very unsubtle interpretation of that text makes St Martha on its basis the patroness of housewives. Yet that is what she became, and when we find that in St John's Gospel she is also recorded as, on another occasion, serving Jesus at the house in Bethany, calling her a housewife is perhaps justified after all. In Western iconography her symbols are a ladle, a broom, and a bunch of keys, which taken together convey a somewhat depressing sense of drudgery combined with domestic control.

Yet, as we know, home-making is a great art, and it is fitting that it has a saint to represent it, since every real home is a kind of sacrament of heaven, our true home. Or, to put it another way, heaven is home relieved of finitude, of limits that narrow sympathy. Without homes there can be no hospitality, and that too is Martha's charism. Hospitality mirrors a divine action, because God in making us makes us precisely guests at the table of creation.

In the Incarnation and the Holy Eucharist, however, God became not only our host but also this time *our* guest at the table of human society. This is the mystery of the Eternal, the Unconditioned, entering time, entering reciprocal relations. And at the heart of that mystery stands today's saint.

30 July, St Peter Chrysologus

'The righteous will shine like the sun in the Kingdom of the Father.' If one wishes to see that particular biblical verse portrayed, there's no better place in the world to go than to Ravenna. There, on the Adriatic coast of Italy, for centuries the main point of contact between Byzantium and the West, you have the righteous before you in shining mosaic, the saints streaming along the lateral walls of the early basilicas towards, in each case, the sanctuary which, within the sacred space of a church building, stands for the Kingdom of heaven.

They beckon us towards glory. 'O sages standing in God's holy fire/ As in the gold mosaic of a wall; come from the holy fire', pleaded the poet Yeats, 'and be the singing-master of my soul./ Consume my heart away; sick with desire/ And fastened to a dying animal/ It knows not what it is'. And he went on to ask the righteous to gather him 'into the artifice of eternity'. It had to be an artifice. That was the only way Yeats could imagine he might become glorious—through his poetry, not in himself, then, not in his full personal reality. That was all he could say because he didn't know, not in the interior way faith implies, what the Incarnation was about.

The Incarnation was the great theme of St Peter Chrysologus, the fifth century bishop of Ravenna whose memorial we keep today. Peter stressed how there is a wonder even more marvellous than art, or than any earthly beauty. And that is the wonder of the Incarnation when, as he put it: 'the hand [of God[that graciously elevated mud into our form [at the creation of man] has now [in the Incarnation] elevated flesh also [by uniting it to himself] for our restoration'. Sick with desire, fastened to a dying animal, the heart knows not what it is. The singing-master, St Peter the Man of the Golden Words, tells our heart: the heart is made for God, made for the vision of God, flesh and spirit, and by the grace of the Incarnation the whole man can be gathered into eternity.

31 July, St Ignatius Loyola

Today is the memorial of St Ignatius Loyola, the founder of the Jesuits, of all Religious Orders surely the most maligned. Ignatius was a Basque soldier and courtier. While convalescing from a cannonball injury, he was converted to a life of radical discipleship through reading the lives of Christ and the saints, where he discovered an alternative sort of heroism.

His original intention and that of the little group of comrades he gathered about him, was simply to live a life of poverty and chastity. But you can't fill in the twenty four hours by just being poor and chaste. So, seeking some more concrete form of God's will they vowed to go on pilgrimage to the Holy Land, or, if travel conditions in the Eastern Mediterranean should make that impossible, to form themselves into a society in the apostolic service of the pope. In this sense, it was the outbreak of war between Venice and the Turks which made possible the Jesuit Order.

Despite, or because of, the formidable missionary, educational and artistic achievements of the Society, their enemies proliferated. By a supreme irony, the Papacy to whose service they were specially vowed, carried through their suppression just before the French Revolution: as the pope of the time put it, 'on grounds suggested to us by the principles of prudence and which remain concealed within our breast'. The loss of this gifted and flexible body of men on the eve of the Revolutionary period was a disaster for the Church, hardly compensated by the restoration of the Society in the post-Revolutionary period. In more recent years, the Jesuits have undergone a certain degree of disorientation in the aftermath of the Second Vatican Council.

There is comfort for them, however, in the thought that the heart of St Ignatius's own spirituality lay in the discernment of the will of God in concrete circumstances. The practice of his *Exercises* with their call for untiring self-criticism in the universal service of Christ the King, should make the Jesuits good at learning from their mistakes. By the intercession of St Ignatius may we all learn from them in this at least.

AUGUST

1 August, St Alphonsus

Alphonsus de Liguori was born near Naples in 1696. He had been a barrister, and losing his most important case seems to have been a turning point in his life. It was a complicated case about feudal tenure where a key phrase bore different senses depending on whether you had in mind the Lombard or the Angevin element in Neapolitan law. (Eighteenth century Naples was full of lawyers partly because its law was so complex, so many different rulers having passed through.) To the irritation of his father, a tough captain of galley slaves, Alphonsus turned his back on the law altogether and by now in his late 20s began to study for the priesthood.

It must be said that he was no luckier when it came to the canon law, rather than the civil jurisdictions. Some six years after Ordination he founded a society of priests, the Congregation of the Most Holy Redeemer ('Redemptorists'), to preach in rural parishes that had been neglected by bishops and local clergy. But owing to a conflict over the documents which granted the new body the right to function (he had allowed others to use his signature without checking what they were signing), he found himself papally excluded for some years from the very society he had created.

I have the impression he was somewhat accident-prone. On one occasion he wrote to the French rationalist philosopher Voltaire congratulating him on his conversion to Catholicism, which of course never happened. And in 1775, by then a bishop, and believing himself to be dying, he resigned his see, whereas in point of fact he lived on for another twelve years, dying in 1787.

His life was nevertheless in ministerial terms extremely fruitful. He brought back to the practice of the faith large numbers of the lapsed, concentrating on the most despised elements in society: the goatherds of the countryside behind Naples, a byword for ignorance and squalor. As a bishop he was tirelessly interventionist whenever there were cases that smacked of scandal or negligence among priests. And all the time he kept up the stream of practical-ly-oriented writing that has made him a doctor of the Church: Catholic apologetics, treatises for confessors, books on how to develop the devout life.

Despite serious problems with scrupulosity, which he could only overcome by promising absolute obedience to spiritual directors, St Alphonsus had, paradoxically, a rather reckless, self-abandoning, side to him which people found occasionally maddening but more often attractive. This was not just personal chemistry as we can tell from the way his devotional life centred on the Eucharistic Christ and the Blessed Virgin. Jesus and Mary are the figures in whom we see self-emptying divinely embodied (in our Lord) or graciously represented (in our Lady).

Self-abandonment, then: it proved possible for him, and if so then perhaps who knows? it is also possible for us.

4 August, St John Vianney

The saying has it, A prophet is not without honour save in his own country. That seems belied by the life of St John Vianney. He got a great deal of honour, eventually, in his own country, if not only there.

At first sight, he looks an unlikely candidate for honours. The son of a small farmer from an off-the-track area of south-eastern France, he was an indifferent student; a deserter from Napoleon's army; admitted to Holy Orders only with great difficulty owing to his lack of academic aptitude. And he spent the rest of his life as a curé in a French village.

But of course it was what happened in the village that made the difference.

To evangelise a collection of dechristianised French peasants and bring them to the fervent practice of religion was already quite something. But it didn't make Jean-Marie famous on a national and even European scale. That was done by the stream of conver-sions which flowed from his confessional, an apostolate that worked as it did owing to his uncanny ability to read hearts.

The technical name for this is 'gnoseocardia': supernaturally enabled access to what is going on in people's hearts, what really makes them tick. John Vianney had a penetration of people that was not only personal but circumstantial with details included. Of course that goes utterly beyond our natural capacities of judgment.

The Fourth Evangelist says of our Lord, 'He knew what was in a man'. That gives us a clue. There is an imitation of Christ in this gift. The booking office set up in the Gare Centrale at Lyons for the three hundred people who daily took the train to see him makes us marvel at the sheer scale of this activity which far exceeded that of the incarnate Word himself. The latter had said to the disciples, after all, of the actions of his own ministry, 'Greater works than these you will do in my name'.

Why? There must have been some Providential reason. We are not let into these secrets but we can speculate. It was the beginning of the period when natural science was to dominate culture, as it does today, and to become the paradigm of knowledge in relation to which both faith and metaphysics were judged and found wanting. John Vianney's life showed that the methods of the natural sciences have their limits.

In the twentieth century, on the eve of an age when the Catholic priesthood in Europe reached the nadir of its fortunes and reputation, he was made the patron of the secular clergy. Such a patron, such a life, is very necessary now.

6 August, The Transfiguration of the Lord (1)

In the Byzantine church, today's festivity is counted one of the twelve Great Feasts. In the West it has not been given such prominence, though Pope Paul VI had the good taste to die on it. It is of course a feast in honour of the glory of God which broke through visibly in the features of Jesus Christ as he stood before his disciples on the hill-top which tradition identifies as Mount Thabor.

But it's not just that, if we wish, we can wax theological about today's feast. Rather, this feast is in a sense *the foundation of all theology*. Theology begins with the flooding of the mind by the Uncreated Light and the concentration of the heart on the person of the Saviour. This is what today's festival shows us. We do not create the foundation of theology. Instead, we rest upon it, and live within its radiance.

The Transfiguration, then, is not so much a feast to think about as a feast to be happy on, a feast to exult in, because it is filled with the beauty, the love, and the joy of God. These have now come within our reach in Jesus Christ our Friend and Brother. We can say as truly of it as we can of Easter (of which it forms the anticipation in the public ministry of our Lord): 'This is the day which the Lord has made. Let us be glad and rejoice in it'.

6 August, The Transfiguration of the Lord (2)

We keep today as a feast one of the two great 'theophanies' or appearances of the triune God in the life of Jesus as presented by the New Testament witnesses. The other is the Baptism of Christ, with which it has certain similarities. Both feasts have been more richly explored in the Christian East. And just as the Baptism of Christ has a special cachet in the Ethiopian liturgy, so the Byzantine liturgy has gone to town on the Transfiguration. It is in the Greek East especially that today's celebration has inspired countless icons and much liturgical poetry and where it is reckoned one of the twelve 'Great Feasts' of the Church.

The Byzantine Fathers stress how the Transfiguration is a manifestation of Christ's glory, of the uncreated splendour of the Logos, which broke through on Mount Thabor, giving the disciples a momentary perception of the divine Energies shared by Father and Spirit with the Son. This is what was now reflected in the radiance of the face of Christ, on his body, and even on his clothing.

From there it may seem a natural move to contrast with this a Western Catholicism centred on—some would say more unkindly, obsessed by—the Cross: the Passion and Death of Christ, the penalty exacted by divine justice for the sins of the world. And yet when we put the various Gospel accounts together, we soon see it isn't as simple as that. The topic of the conversational exchange between Jesus, Moses and Elijah, is, as St Luke tells us, Jesus' forthcoming Passion. Moses and Elijah embody the holy warfare of the struggle with evil (with Pharaoh in the one case, with Jezebel and the gods of Canaan in the other). So they are suitable presences for the events of the Last Days: our Lord's final confrontation with Satan, with sin and with death. And when, as St Matthew and St Mark report, Jesus goes on, after the vision has passed, to predict his approaching death and to caution the disciples not to tell what they have seen until his sufferings are completed, what does this signify if not an intimate connexion between the glory and the Cross?

So what is that intimate connexion? The glory of the Son, as of the Father and the Holy Spirit, is ultimately the glory of love: the sovereign yet sacrificial love which not only saved the world in the events that founded our religion but also made the world in the first place when God shared being with what was not himself. And this love, furthermore, not only made (and saved) the world but also constitutes the world's Maker in his own Trinitarian life before time was thanks to the mutual self-giving of the divine Persons. As the poet Hopkins puts it, the life of the Trinity is everlasting sacrifice.

Without the Cross, then, we can't interpret correctly the glory of the Transfiguration. It is on Calvary that we find the supreme illustration of the Father's words, 'This is my beloved Son'. One sometimes seems crucifixes where the artist, to show Christ reigning gloriously from the Tree, has given him a crown to wear. But really the crucifix needs no crown; the mangled limbs of the Saviour are already his glorious regalia. The Resurrection, when it comes, will not cancel out the Crucifixion. Instead it will display the truth of the Crucifixion, its grace and its power.

8 August, St Dominic

About the profile of St Dominic here is a certain impersonality, and even abstractness. The reason generally given is, he was swallowed up in his work. His work absorbed his particularity since his life was given over to the task he had set himself: starting off a new evangelical way of life, forming an Order of Preachers. That was to be the 'face' he showed the world.

Preaching the Gospel: how was it to be done? Not mainly by distributing little tracts like Evangelicals in Market Square. Nor chiefly by giving sermons on the liturgical year, as the Orthodox might. Preaching the Gospel was principally to happen through living the apostolic life, as the apostles had lived it with the Lord.

Being sent out to preach, as St Dominic understood it, was an overflow from being with our Lord. Preaching about Jesus would be trivialized if it did not result for preacher and hearer in some intensification of life in Christ. Certainly preaching is hollow for the preacher unless at least episodically it flows from the abundance of contemplation.

We speak rather glibly about 'the Gospel' without always pausing to say what we think it is. Ultimately, it is the Word incarnate in all his dimensions: the mystery of Christ as the source of all the saving truth the Church knows. Yves Congar remarked, 'There is Gospel where Jesus Christ is present and active to communicate life'. So the apostolic life as Dominic built it into the Order of Preachers means being with the Saviour at depth—at such a depth that it should be impossible not to speak about him.

Following St Dominic's intention, this means in the first place a liturgical life, a life that revolves around the celebration of the Mass and the Liturgy of the Hours. He was, after all, a canon regular. But there wasn't just piety in the house, there was also hard work. Largely, the role of manual labour in monasticism was now replaced by study, seen as part of the ascetical way, and even the mystical way, the way of moral and spiritual purification with a view to growth in union with God.

On the feast of St Dominic, however, it may be more appropriate to remember what will remain when the hard slog of study is over, the work of preaching complete and only shared delight in God left. The Christian life, as St Thomas urges, is about happiness, a blessed happiness. And it should begin to be tangible even now. Each should be able to say about his holy house, *Hic domus Dei et porta caeli*: 'This is [for me] the house of God and the gate of heaven'. Or if not, then why not?

9 August, St Teresa Benedicta of the Cross

St Teresa Benedicta of the Cross was born in Breslau, in Prussia, to an orthodox Jewish family of business people, in 1891. She was born on the eve of Yom Kippur, the Day of Atonement, or, as Jews call it, 'Expiations' or 'the Great Pardon'. That is relevant to her destiny.

During her education it transpired that she was what the Germans term *ein Wunderkind*: she was super-endowed with intellectual talent. At some point in her youth she became bored by the Synagogue services and drifted off into religious indifference, and eventually atheism. It was her discovery, first, of the difference Christian faith made to newly widowed friends from the years of the First World War and, secondly, of the autobiography of St Teresa of Avila, the reformer of Carmel, that made her seek out Baptism in the Catholic Church. This she did on New Year's Day, 1921. She was twenty-nine.

Despite the demands of war-work as a medical orderly, she was launched on an academic career in philosophy. She had been, after all, the professional assistant of Edmund Husserl, founder of the philosophical movement called 'phenomenology'. Deemed a 'new Scholasticism' for its stress on the importance of things as they are in themselves, it would shape the thinking of the most influential of modern popes, John Paul II. But Edith had also been thinking very hard about God and not just about the world. Through her Baptism she re-discovered the faith of her people, Israel.

But it was not for this she had sought Baptism (she was not simply a 'reverting' Jewess). She had become a Christian, and more specifically a Catholic Christian, and she had done so, by her own admission, so that she might enter 'Carmel'. She proposed to take on the austere life of following Jesus Christ in humility and poverty which characterizes the sacrificial life of the enclosed nuns of the Carmelite Order, with their link via the hermits of Mount Carmel to the prophet Elijah and thereby to the history of the Old Testament people of God.

In April 1933 legislation removed all persons of Jewish origin from posts in higher education. Edith took this to be the Providential sign she had been waiting for and, to the dismay of her family, entered the Carmel of Cologne, adopting a deliberately punning name in religion 'Teresa blessed by the Cross', which could also be rendered 'Teresa Benedicta of the Cross' and indeed during her teaching years she had struck up a close link with the Benedictine abbey of Beuron, a pioneer of the liturgical revival. Contrary to what might be expected, the Carmel, which had no intellectual pretensions, not only permitted but encouraged her to carry on with her philosophical writing, and she now produced her chief work, 'Finite and Eternal Being', as well as an interpretation of the mystical theology of St John of the Cross, 'The Science of the Cross'.

She would soon need that science herself because the Nazi net was closing on all Jews. She was moved to another Carmel across the Dutch border out of harm's way, so it was thought, but in 1940 Germany invaded the Netherlands. She already had clear intimations that she was to die as a sacrificial offering for the rejection of the Gospel by the Jewish people, for the future of the Church in Germany, and for the world. Negotiations to have her transferred to a Carmel in neutral Switzerland were so protracted by administrative red-tape that time ran out. The open letter of the Dutch bishops protesting against the deportation of the Jews of the Netherlands triggered in reprisal a Nazi round-up of specifically Catholic Jews (this is an important part of the claim that Edith Stein died as a martyr). She was permitted to keep her habit so long as she sewed a yellow star of David onto it. With her sister Rosa, who had followed her into the Church and was a Carmelite tertiary, she was dispatched to the notorious Auschwitz extermination centre. She entered there into the heritage of her birthday, Yom Kippur. Among her last recorded words were those to her sister as guards hustled them away, 'Come, let us go for our people'.

10 August, St Laurence

St Laurence's story is set in the middle of the third century during one of the worst phases of persecution of the ancient Church at Rome. The pope had already been arrested and sentenced to death. As he was going out to the place of execution, Laurence called out to him: 'Father, where are you going without your deacon?' To this the pope replied prophetically that Laurence would follow him in three days' time.

Ever since the case of St Ignatius of Antioch at the end of the first Christian century, the words of a bishop on his way to martyrdom have been given special weight. So Laurence believed him, and spent the intervening hours dispensing the monies of the

Church to the Roman poor, notably to widows and orphans (in those days, deacons acted as treasurers of the churches). The Roman prefect heard of this sudden flood of money which obviously implied the Church had considerable wealth and contacted Laurence, requiring him to hand over the 'treasure of the Church'. Laurence then rounded up the beneficiaries of his almsgiving, and, so the story goes, arranged them in rows: the blind, the lame, the maimed, lepers, orphans and so on, and then invited the prefect to inspect the 'treasury'. Not unnaturally this produced an apoplectic outburst from the prefect who promised Laurence would not get away lightly with this insult to the State. He would die by inches, which suggested, then, turning on the gridiron: an iron bed to which the victim was strapped, coals burning beneath. Modern times can show as well as ancient that pathological political action often gets joined to a sick imagination and produces ingenious horrors.

Two points seem to arise from this narrative. The first concerns the treasure of the Church. Yes, the materially poor can be treasures of the Church. But let us not forget those who are what our Lord calls 'the poor in spirit'. Everywhere in the Church there should be hidden saints.

Secondly, the prophetic words of Pope Sixtus to Laurence spoke of 'three days' until his martyrdom. Three days is the time-lapse between Good Friday and Easter. It is, as we say in Holy Week, the 'triduum' of our salvation. We might suppose that Laurence's ghastly death was his Good Friday not his Easter. But the Office Hymn for the feasts of martyrs' celebrates their death-days as their 'triumph day', their Eastertide. The death of a martyr harvests the fruit of the Paschal suffering and victory of Christ. The martyrs know that their deaths are, thanks to Christ, their entry into glory.

11 August, St Clare

Is the reality of Christianity today chiefly a *factum*, something already achieved: in plain English, a fact? Or is it mainly an *agendum*, a project or programme to be carried out: in fairly plain English, an agenda? Put in very basic terms: is the Christian life first and foremost contemplative and celebratory, or is it primarily active and agitatory?

It is too important a question to be shrugged off as a matter of different religious temperaments or papered over by appeals for moderation and balance. It can only be answered in terms of theological doctrine—how we understand our relation to creation and redemption.

Is creation mainly to be received with gratitude and dwelt in accordingly? Or is to be regarded as just the starting-point of transformation by man? And likewise, is redemption something objectively achieved by the saving Incarnation and all its consequences up to the Resurrection and the descent of the Holy Spirit? Or do the texts which tell us of these things simply locate a promise which is to be cashed only at the end of history and which in the meantime we live out by the practice of hope?

In terms of these sets of alternatives St Clare of Assisi belongs firmly to the first in each case. Creation and redemption are vast facts to be savoured in a life-long contemplation which is by itself a sufficient reason for existing. Touched by the preaching of St Francis, Clare sold all her possession and moved into the little house next to the church of San Damiano in Assisi which Francis had restored. She never left it again except on two occasions when, during sieges of the town, she was carried to the walls to pray. Her life was filled with wonder at the world of nature and with humble praise in the face of salvation: those features that give early Franciscanism its lyrical quality, which is at once cosmic and evangelical.

But what does the life of such a saint have to say to the needs expressed in the second pair of terms in the sets of alternatives I put before you? Basically, the contemplative and celebratory life which is primary creates the ethos that makes activity Christian. No attempt at transforming the world or society which ignores this ethos will rise above activism, whereas with this ethos action becomes mission, a prolonging of the sending of the Son and the Spirit from the eternal Father to whom, through them, all things will return.

14 August, St Maximilian Kolbe

Maximilian Kolbe is one of the Polish saints added to the Calendar by Blessed John Paul II. At the time of the Solidarity movement, the figure of St Maximilian was briefly presented to viewers of television in England: not, however, as a martyr, which is how the Church celebrates him today, but as the planner and builder of the so-called 'City of the Immaculate' from where his fellow-Franciscans launched a media-inspired campaign to spread Catholic doctrine, spirituality and social ideals, using all the resources of the technology of the period the inter-War years while pursuing a life of fervent ascetical and indeed mystical commitment.

Why the Church raised him to the altars was not, though, chiefly for this. Rather, it was principally for the single action whereby in the exercise yard at Auschwitz he stepped forward to offer himself as a substitute for the life of a young husband and father whom the prison authorities had just condemned to death in a random reprisal. We are dealing here with an act of substitution which recalls and in some way perpetuates the primal act of substitution whereby mankind's Head and Representative, Jesus Christ, offered himself on the Cross in the place of all. So it is a martyrdom that raises the question of the character of human solidarity and its relation to Christ.

When at the Incarnation, the Son of God assumed our nature and became consubstantial with us, he did not just become another member of the human species. More than that, he entered into a potential union with each and every human being in becoming the New Adam, the new Head of the human race. And when we ourselves are incorporated into him by Baptism and the Eucharist we cease to be related to others as simply fellow members of a species. Instead, we begin actually to share in this mystery of solidarity in the New Adam. That solidarity or what the lay theologian Charles Williams used to call 'the co-inherence' finds its expression above all in a life of charity. And charity can either be, as is more usual, a matter of active self-giving, or it can be, as in martyrdom, a passive self-giving. To become a victim of charity was St Maximilian's way of bearing witness in his dying to the new solidarity of all human beings in our Lord.

15 August, Solemnity of the Assumption (1)

'The Queen stands at your right hand, arrayed in gold' was the
response to the gradual psalm of today's Mass. With considerable
boldness, the Roman Liturgy applies to today's Solemnity this text
from an ancient Israelite wedding song probably written for the
marriage of the rather dodgy king Ahab to the quite unspeakable
princess Jezebel. The Queen, Mary, stands at the right hand of the
King, Christ, in glory. These words give us a clue, however, to the
thinking or intuition behind today's feast and the extraordinary
event of which that thinking or intuition is an echo. The clue lies
in the closeness, the intimacy, of Mary and Christ. The Gospels
portray Mary as closely joined to her divine Son, and drawn into
his lot.

A constant theme of the New Testament, and especially of the
Letters of St Paul, is the way in which union with Christ in his
saving death brings about union with him in his Resurrection. We
co-suffer with him so as to be co-glorified; and this sense of *union
leading to participation* is so strong in Paul especially that he strains
the resources of the Greek language to express it, coining all sorts
of new words with the little syllable *syn*: meaning 'co-' ('with' or
'together with') tacked on in front rather as in our words 'synchro-
nise' or 'syncopate'. What the Church says of our Lady is that she
so intimately suffered with her Son, above all at the foot of Calvary,
that she equally intimately reigned with him, standing at his right
hand, arrayed in gold.

This follows the logic of all Christian salvation. If we are
historically justified in celebrating a feast of the Sorrows of Mary,
the grieving Mother, *Mater dolorosa,* she who stood by the Cross in
every sense of that pregnant phrase to 'stand by someone' (and,
to judge by the New Testament, we *are* historically justified in
doing that), then we must also be doctrinally justified in celebrating
a feast of Mary's Assumption, her complete and definitive entry
into the glory of her Son.

Mary's Assumption is not, however, a personal privilege
irrespective of any wider function for her, a function that might,
say, concern ourselves. In the work of salvation, there are no such
privileges devoid of responsibilities; no gifts given that do not

imply duties; no *noblesse* that does not *oblige*. There is no sharing in the divine life that does not produce the most characteristic sign of that life: namely, self-giving. Mary's glorification is in one sense the end of her life, but it another sense it is only its beginning. It is her entry upon her duties in the regime of glory, the regime of transfiguration by which the world becomes the Church, and the Church the Kingdom, when sinful humanity becomes the company of the redeemed, and the evil and mediocre are turned into saints.

At the Assumption, Mary initiates the activity prophesied by her dying Son when he gave his Mother to the infant Church expressed in the Beloved Disciple and did so with the words, 'This is your Mother'. It is because of the Assumption that we can call on Mary as not only Mother of God but Mother of the Church, and call for her to exercise her motherhood with efficacy in our regard, so that through her we may be allowed to glimpse the glory in which she is bathed, the radiance of the uncreated Love which shines out in the face of her risen Son.

15 August, Solemnity of the Assumption (2)

When I was in the Caucasus, I was told a story that is relevant to today's Solemnity. When the Russians took over Georgia and abolished the East Georgian monarchy in 1810, they were worried about possible future disaffection. So they took the Bagratids, the royal family, to St Petersburg, in order to keep an eye on them there. Now the Bagratids were proud of their claimed descent in the direct line from king Solomon. On the feast of the Assumption the Falling Asleep of the Mother of God, as the Orthodox call it, the court of St Petersburg was surprised to find the Bagratid princesses dressed in the colours of mourning. 'Whatever has happened?', they enquired. 'Oh, don't you know', the Georgians said to the Russians, 'there's been a death in the family'.

As Catholics we also would be surprised, because the death of the Virgin is not just 'a death', one among many. As deaths go, it's absolutely unique, and absolutely unique in such a way that it becomes an occasion for celebration, not lamentation. The Virgin did not need to die as we die. As the Immaculate, she didn't belong to the moral order or, rather, disorder, of this world. She wasn't subject to the kind of death that is the outcome of the present moral disorder: after the Fall, I mean. She died the death we die only because she freely chose it. As the Mother of the Saviour she freely chose to follow the way of her Son.

That's what the Byzantine Liturgy tells us at Matins of today's feast.

> If the Fruit she bore [i. e. Christ], by whose favour she passes to heaven, freely endured the tomb insofar as he is mortal, how can she refuse the tomb, she who unwedded bore the Child?

Mary died as we do because it is congruent with the Christ-pattern to do so. It's all of a piece with his life and hers: giving, self-giving, in humility, sacrifice, self-abandonment. And this is also why she is glorified by being taken to heaven body and soul. Her manner of dying was the final seal on her holiness, the ultimate seal, and so it had, in her Assumption and Coronation, the ultimate reward.

Yet still it goes on: her mediation with her Son, her offering herself as a channel of his graces, lavished on others. That is part and parcel of the pattern too. The French have a saying for it: *noblesse oblige*. Nobility sets up obligations. And that holds good in Christian doctrine as well. The higher the degree of glory a creature receives, the heavier is its responsibility, its responsibility to communicate the divine goodness occasionally, at least to others. We ask to be made holy. But do we always realize to what we are committing ourselves? In the communion of saints, there is no private holiness. That is also included in the message today.

15 August, Solemnity of the Assumption (3)

It was in November 1950 that Pope Pius XII made the Assumption of Mary, the feast we celebrate today, a dogma binding all Catholic Christians to their assent in faith. To celebrate Mary's Assumption is now part and parcel of what it means to be a Catholic. If you called yourself a Catholic and didn't assent in faith to the Assumption you would be inventing a private definition of what the word 'Catholic' means. To be a Catholic is to celebrate the Assumption.

Now to declare something a dogma, binding on all Christians in this way, is obviously an unusual sort of thing to do. Popes and

Councils don't go round doing this just to pass the time or keep their hands in. Dogma belongs to the Church's communication of God's call to each of us. It is one way in which the love of God asks for our attention and invites our response. So if there are dogmas about Mary, that can only be because the figure of Mary somehow belongs to the whole plan of God for our salvation. There can't, then, be a full flowering of our Christian lives unless by faith and love we recognize what Mary means in the work of salvation, unless we recognize a special relationship with her.

So what does the Assumption mean? In one sense, what it means is very obvious. It means that at a particular place and time the physical body of a particular woman passed through death to life, as the eternal and only God took her to himself. And the first thing *that* implies is the material embodiment of salvation. On paper, in the abstract, in poetry, in imagery, the union of the Heavenly with the Earthly, or the Glorification of the Feminine Principle, is all very fine. But the highly concrete and specific claim that we have to look to the transformed body of one Palestinian-Jewish woman, now sharing in the new life of the risen Christ, to find out what human life is all about and where it's going: this is rather different.

In fact, it is the beauty of the Assumption dogma, the Assumption festival. Today's Solemnity proclaims the significance of the particular, the significance of matter, the significance of the flesh. It saves us from the proud idealism or spiritual high-mindedness which refuses to allow that God can really mean to save us *in the flesh*. The Assumption dogma was proclaimed so as to recall modern men and women to a true sense of the destiny and holiness of matter. It was proclaimed to save us from that little voice within us that whispers how true religion is only spiritual and the flesh leads to corruption. It was proclaimed to save us from the exploitation of the body for sex or money in the oppression of others. The true wholeness of the body is now seen in the Virgin Mother whose body was the temple of the living Word. That same flesh of the Mother of Christ now belongs to God's finished creation. It is in her flesh that all emotions and desires, all the secret sources of instinct and awareness, and all the conscious movements of the knower and the lover, have been gathered into blessedness.

God is saving us through the Church of his Son, and the beacon
of our common life in Christ is Mary. She shows us that vision of
God in which the whole human being is called to perfection.

17 August, St Hyacinth

St Hyacinth was one of the major figures in the far-reaching
thirteenth century expansion of Latin Christendom. He was born
in Silesia in 1185, became a Dominican, probably in Rome, about
1217, and fixed his missionary base at Cracow in Poland. He
appears to have evangelized over a huge area from Gdansk to Kiev,
from Lithuania to the Black Sea. He was part of the high mediaeval
attempt to Christianise Russia where by 1600 the Dominicans had
seventy houses, at least three of them beyond the Dnieper in Great
Russia itself.

In 1238 much, perhaps most, of Hyacinth's work was destroyed
by the Mongol invasions. Until his death in 1257 he spent the rest
of his life picking up the pieces. The mission of the Church is rather
like the stone of Sisyphus, pushed up the slope even as it falls down
again. Our fidelity to the Gospel is measured often by dogged
persistence.

20 August, St Bernard

St Bernard was born about 1030 near Dijon in Burgundy. As a
young man he is described as charming, witty, learned and
eloquent: qualities which, had he been born nine hundred years
later, would have made him the perfect guest at a cocktail party.
But he must have been more than this to persuade thirty-one of
his uncles, brothers and cousins to join him in applying to enter a
local monastery, dwindling in numbers but ultra-austere: Citeaux,
from whose name we get the word 'Cistercian'.

After a few years probation Bernard became abbot of Clairvaux,
a new foundation with which his name will always be linked and
from where he, in effect, re-founded the Cistercian Order and
exerted unparalleled influence over the Western church of his day.

St Bernard's causes were those of the twelfth century Gregorian
reform: reforming the life-style of the clergy, especially by the
ending of clerical concubinage; defending doctrinal orthodoxy;

supporting the Crusades; strengthening the Petrine office as the necessary instrument for gaining these other ends, and doing all this through, not least, the placing of fervent Cistercian monks in positions of influence, a process whose high point was the election of one such monk as Pope Eugenius III.

It may come as a surprise, given all these tough-minded pursuits, that the mystical theology of Bernard, for which he was declared a doctor of the Church, is centred entirely on the love of God, understood in a very human way that is curiously modern by which I mean feminine or at least soft. God is to be loved, since it is by love that human powers are most deeply engaged. Bernard's achievement was to transfer to the life of faith the insights into courtly love typical of the troubadours, and thus to play his part in the clearer identification of a central feature of the Gospel: the love of God for us, and the corresponding love this arouses in us for him.

In this Bernard had a notable influence in the Church, not least on St Thomas Aquinas. When Thomas was stricken on the road to the General Council about to open at Lyons, he asked to be taken to the Cistercian abbey of Fossanova, which he seems to have chosen quite consciously as his last dwelling place. It is Bartholomew of Capua who tells us that as he arrived there Thomas clutched at the doorpost of the monastery, reciting as he did so Psalm 131, the fourteenth verse of which runs, 'This is my resting place for ever; here have I chosen to dwell'.

As he lay dying, the Cistercians asked him a little unfairly, perhaps, to give them a brief commentary on their favourite biblical book, which was the Song of Songs. According to Cistercian tradition, Thomas replied, 'If I can have the spirit of Bernard, I will'. St Bernard's homilies on the Song of Songs cover a lengthy period of his life. So what Bernard did his whole life long, Thomas did in the end.

If Thomas' commentary were ever written down it has since been lost. But it is easy to find out what was the 'spirit of Bernard' from Bernard's own texts. His sermons take their starting-point and indeed their whole structure and their tone from the Song's opening words, 'Let him kiss me with the kiss of his mouth'. As we know, a kiss is a sign of oneness, and in the case of a kiss on the lips, of intimate oneness. For Bernard this kiss is Jesus Christ, the Mediator between God and man who joins the 'mouths' of divinity and humanity in his own person, but beyond even the humanity assumed by the Word, the kiss is, going deeper still, the Holy Spirit who joins Father and Son in the eternal Godhead. If we say, 'Let him kiss me with the kiss of his mouth', what we are saying is that we aspire to a union with Christ the Lord in the Holy Spirit.

But Bernard warns we cannot go straight at such intimate union. We have to move towards it by two intermediate stages: what he terms 'the kiss of the feet', which means conversion and repentance, and 'the kiss of the hand', the divine hand which reaches down to lift us up, and this means relying on God's strength in whatever good actions we carry out in a spirit of praise and thanks. Only then are we to seek the kiss of the mouth or what Bernard calls the 'kiss of infinite condescension and indescribable sweetness'.

This progression from the feet, to the hand, to the lips: this, surely, is what Thomas will have meant by commenting the Song in the spirit of Bernard.

Since St Thomas, who died in a Cistercian monastery composing a commentary on the Song of Songs in the spirit of St Bernard, Dominicans have not, I think, shown any special interest in this teacher. That is due in part, I'm afraid, to the disassociation of sensibility which began to separate theological thinking from spirituality in Scholasticism after the high Middle Ages. Perhaps the time has come to make honourable amends, for we need a thought that is intensely religious and a religion that is genuinely thoughtful, placed in the service of a total vision of the Church as the loving Bride of Jesus Christ.

We cannot be content with a merely rational theology, a theology consisting of thinking about God. We need to have a mystical theology, a theology of lived union with him. In a sense, Thomas's last words to his readers were: Go to Bernard. Advice definitely worth heeding.

21 August, St Pius X

Pius X was born plain Giuseppe Sarto, Joseph Taylor, in 1835 in a village of the Venetian plain, then part of the Austrian Empire. His father was the local postman, but this did not prevent Giuseppe from becoming in succession chancellor of the local diocese, bishop of Mantua and patriarch of Venice. Where the Council of Trent had failed, nineteenth century Ultramontanism succeeded, and this was in breaking the link between high social connexions and clerical promotion.

In 1903 he became pope, thanks partly to the veto cast against his rival by his father's employer, Franz Josef, exercising for the last time that prerogative of a Western emperor in the Church.

Pius X's pontificate is something of a mystery to liberal critics. On the one hand, he was an 'advanced' pope, who tried to return the Liturgy to the people, encouraging fuller ritual participation in the Mass and frequent Communion, even for children. He also urged lay-people to take a great share in the apostolate. On the other hand, during the Modernist crisis, he was exceedingly severe in the canonical penalties he attached to theological error, seeing the heresies of heresies in the movement of thought and scholarship dubbed 'Modernism', according to which doctrinal formulae should be used when they are found helpful to the articulation of religious experience but otherwise discarded.

Possibly not all St Pius's decisions were invariably prudent. That is not a precondition for the recognition of sanctity. But he had certainly taken to heart the following words of St Paul: 'The Gospel we preached to you is no human invention. If anyone, be he an angel of God, preach to you a different Gospel from that you have received from us, let him be anathema. We give thanks for you because when you heard the Gospel we preached to you, you received it as what it is, the Word of God and not the words of men.'

22 August, The Queenship of the Blessed Virgin Mary

One important way in which the Church expresses her sense of who Mary is comes in the form of titles such as Mary the Queen. A wit once said that the Church of England is the only Church in

Christendom where the phrase 'our most gracious Sovereign Lady' does *not* refer to the Blessed Virgin Mary. This title is old in Latin (*regina, domina*) and in Greek (*basilissa, despoina*) but its oldest appearance of all is in a language closely related to our Lord's own, Syriac, in the fourth century.

In the Latin church this title became familiar to mediaeval Christians through hymns like the *Salve regina* and the *Regina caeli*. In the Litany of Loreto Mary is appealed to as Queen in as many as twelve different ways. So there was an extensive background when in 1954 Pope Pius XII created a feast of Mary the Queen for the Roman rite.

The imagery of our Lady's Queenship derives, of course, from the practice of monarchy in traditional societies. Unlike today, a queen was a genuinely powerful person. Also unlike today, in a smaller scale world, she was an accessible, available person. Like the king, the queen made power human through being reachable by petitioners or suppliants, people with grievances or complaints, people with ideas or enthusiasms, the good, bad, and indifferent, the holy or the plain dotty. So devotion to Mary as Queen does not, as some people say, create too great a distance from Mary the Mother. She is always holding court, ready, in the Holy Spirit, to hear and receive the prayers of her Son's disciples and make their cause her own.

It is, after all, Christ who crowns his Mother, and it is from his Kingship as the creative Word through whom all things exist and the New Adam victorious over sin and death that her title derives.

23 August, St Rose of Lima

Occasional glitches apart, the Dominicans have been known in history for the doctrinal solidity of their teaching, backed up by a traditional form of conventual life: sober, liturgical, fraternal. One unforeseen consequence was that all kinds of individuals with a very different approach to holy living have felt drawn into their ambit. Today's saint, Rose of Lima, is a good example.

Dominican spirituality is about intellectual contemplation on the one hand and the virtue of fortitude in preaching the Gospel on the other. It puts faith to use by study and reflection while asking for supernatural Wisdom from the Holy Spirit and the courage to pass on the fruits of contemplation to others.

It has little to do with living as a hermit in a hut in one's father's garden, practicing extreme mortification such as putting rocks and broken glass into one's bed, and spending hours in church largely unconscious in prolonged rapture, goggled at by crowds. Yet this is what Rose, Dominican tertiary, born in 1586, dying in 1617, did.

She is not by any means the only example of this sort of thing, either among the laywomen the Third Order attracted or among the nuns whose monasteries came under its umbrella. Was it opposite poles attracting? Or simply that people with unusual calls to the ascetical and mystical life felt the need for a context that was doctrinally stable and humane?

Anyway, it probably did the friars good. The spiritual fervour these lay women and nuns offered quite likely helped them. After all, St Dominic's own spirit of mortification had gone well beyond the Constitutions of the Order he founded, just as the devotional warmth of his prayer went beyond the spirit of its liturgical life, which was that of canons regular.

No one gets to heaven by mere intellectualism and practicing moderation in all things.

24 August, St Bartholomew

The early Church historian Eusebius reports a tradition that when Pantaenus, the Egyptian theologian who taught the great Origen, went off on a mission to Arabia he found Christians who claimed their community had been founded by St Bartholomew. Those Arab Christians also maintained that the apostle had given their ancestors a copy of the Gospel according to St Matthew in the Hebrew language. The last part has long interested scholars who toy with the idea of a Semitic original for what the Fathers deemed to be the first of the Gospels to be written. Iran, Armenia, the Crimea, and Egypt itself are other places that have put forward a claim to be the scene of Bartholomew's labours, and perhaps that is not far-fetched if, like St Paul, St Bartholomew saw part of his apostolic work as touching down in as many places as possible, so that the Gospel of the Risen Lord to whom all authority was given by the Father could be described—symbolically at least—as preached all over the world.

That Bartholomew was martyred by being flayed alive (in Rome's Sistine Chapel Michelangelo shows him holding up his skin to the viewer) is also quite credible, though it flags up the interesting point that the Church always assumes an apostle to have been a martyr unless, as with St John, proved otherwise. Why, we might ask, is that assumption made?

We could almost say it depended on a pun. People whose job was to hand over, the tradition, the apostolic witness, had themselves to be ready to be 'traditioned', handed over, for the sake of witness to the Gospel just as the Father had given over his only Son into the hands of sinful men for the world's salvation. For the apostles, the deposit of faith (right teaching, orthodoxy) was inseparable from faithfulness to Christ and the form of his mission: to be the servant of God's design until death.

The deaths of the apostles were not just the terminus of their lives. Their deaths were the opportunity for their greatest act of witness, *martyria*, to their common Lord. The Church founded on the apostles is founded on language and on blood.

26 August, Blessed Dominic of the Mother of God

Until John Henry Newman's beatification by Pope Benedict XVI, keeping a memorial day for Blessed Dominic of the Mother of God who received Newman into the Catholic Church was a sort of surrogate for celebrating liturgically Newman himself. Now, however, we must celebrate Blessed Dominic in his own right.

In contrast to Newman's subtle, fastidious, Oxford-donnish mind, Dominic Barberi was a fervent Religious of the Mediterranean sort. He was born in the Papal States, under a theocracy, and affected by the growing Ultramontanism of the Papacy in the wake of the French Revolution. In his own mind, his religious vocation was always bound up with the conversion of England which at first he seems to have identified in imagination with London. In a dream he saw a great city covered in smog, with a thick line of slime running through it, but the darkness cleared when the figure of the pope, carrying the torch of faith, entered the townscape.

In the event, Blessed Dominic's ministry was either to cradle Catholics or to the handful of Oxford converts on the eve of their secession from the Church of England, and it was spent as much in the countryside as in the cities. Ordinary Englishmen, unless cradle Catholics, would have found his way of life outrageous: his insistence on wearing the Passionist habit at all time, his poverty, his Italianate preaching, his emphasis on the confessional. But for the academics, agonizing over the authenticity or otherwise of the Roman primacy clause in St Cyprian's treatise 'On the Unity of the Church', this uncomplicated representative of maximal Catholicism was just what they needed.

So in a way he did not dream of, Blessed Dominic played his not minor part in the Catholic Revival in England.

27 August, St Monica

It's probable that we would never have heard of St Monica if she hadn't been the mother of St Augustine and reflecting why it's worthwhile celebrating *him* belongs with his feast which, not by chance, falls tomorrow.

Augustine's *Confessions* portray her as a formidable woman with an iron determination to get her own way. At one level she was a very possessive mother, so much so that for a while St Ambrose, the eminent bishop of Milan who had been prefect of the city, only remembered Augustine as the son of Monica. It is all summed up in the scene where, having disposed of Augustine's common law wife, she stands at the port with her silent heartbroken son watching the ship taking the girl back to Africa sail out of sight. Naturally, Monica kept her attractive and intelligent grandchild.

But at the port of Ostia where she was eventually buried, Christians kept her cultus alive throughout the dark ages, showing that the instinct of faith recognized in Monica holiness and not just psychological power. As someone has put it, there was a self-transcendence in her very possessiveness: her plan for Augustine was that he should so live as a Christian man that the grace of God, and not Monica, would have the mastery of his turbulent soul and brilliant mind.

And so the penultimate miniature in which Augustine describes her is very apt: the two of them in a shared experience of rapture before God at a window in Ostia. There they stand, the living embodiment of a famous definition of love, which is not to look at each other but to look together in the same direction.

28 August, St Augustine of Hippo

For anyone who dips into the early part of St Augustine's *Confessions*, it's hard to forget the memorable descriptions: Carthage, 'where the cauldron of filthy loves boiled over me'; the singing community gathered by St Ambrose at Milan; the nameless concubine sent, by order of Augustine's mother, back to Africa minus her child. That dramatic prelude comes to an end, however, quickly enough. But though living ever afterwards in fairly humble circumstances in a second rate provincial town, Augustine drew ever more people through his written as well as his spoken words.

I think it had something to do with his gift of sympathy. He combined tenderness with inflexibility in an interesting way. And he recognized very frankly his need for others, his hunger for human company, human exchange. Augustine admired St Anthony of Egypt and the first Christian hermits, but his own vision of the monastic life was essentially one of a gathering of friends in a common search for God, a search where, he considered, he could feel the touch of Christ in the circle of his brethren.

And it is through that conventual context of Augustine's preaching, theological writing, and indeed holiness that Dominicans are related to him related by receiving from him through the canons regular of the early Middle Ages his *Regula ad servos Dei*, a 'Rule for the Servants of God', written originally for a lay monastery but used later in a common life among clerics in the bishop's house at Hippo.

For a theologian's writing or a bishop's preaching to be shaped by a sense of fraternity and friendship has overtones of the communion of knowledge and love between Christ and his disciples articulated most fully in the Farewell Discourse of the Gospel according to St John. On that Discourse Augustine has left us a profound commentary in his *Tractates* on the Fourth Gospel.

And that in turn takes us to the heart of Augustine's *Rule* whose opening chapter begins: 'Before all else you must live together harmoniously, one in heart and one in soul, on the way to God'. In the same chapter Augustine ends, congruently enough, 'Let all of you live together in unity of mind and heart, and honour God in one another'. As he sums up elsewhere, 'Have the one soul of the Church which is mounting towards the peace of unity in the heavenly City'.

This testimony to the shared life which is to generate preaching and teaching is all the more impressive in that it comes from someone who knew that the human story is not a pastoral idyll. The human story is the story of Paradise Lost, and only at great cost is it Paradise Regained. The testimony comes from someone who knew the corrosive capacity of evil and the masquerades of love in the heart. A man who had a vision of all human souls as one mass doomed to loss and falling into perdition in the terrifying mystery of God's permissive will, until God himself takes a hand with the Incarnation of his Son and reveals that he will give his grace to those who, led by his hand, keep to his way.

Augustine has been attacked for excessive pessimism. But can a perception of evil ever be 'excessive'? And can anyone really appreciate justifying grace without some perception of this kind?

Without the bad news of how precariously we are situated, the fragility of goodness, what is the good news of the Gospel worth? We can't keep the precepts of Augustine's *Rule* without also heeding his wisdom. We can't have the fraternal legislator without the doctor of grace.

29 August, The Passion of St John the Baptist

There must be very few things that connect the last Kaiser of Germany to Butler's *Lives of the Saints*. The only one I know is their attitude to the severed head of St John the Baptist. Wilhelm II was so outraged by the scene in Richard Strauss's operatic version of the martyrdom where Strauss has Salome take the head off its platter and caress it that he had the Berlin Opera House production closed down. Alban Butler, an eighteenth century gentleman, had a similar reaction when faced by the head served on a plate.

Though Herod was, he wrote, 'a man of uncommon barbarity', he was shocked at 'the very mention of such a thing by a lady'.

If anyone wishes to write an historical novel, Herod Antipas, the tetrarch of Galilee, would make a good subject. Here is a man torn between respect for a prophet's holiness and fury at John's comments on his domestic arrangements. His deviousness and complexity—our Lord will call him 'that fox'—make Herod humanly interesting to us.

The Church, however, is not interested in human interest, in the play of psycho-dramas. What counts for her in the martyrdom of the Baptist is the way it announces in advance the Passion of the Lord. This is the only martyr's feast we keep under the title, 'The Passion': The Passion of St John, the Forerunner. We name John's sufferings so because they herald the Passion of Christ himself. John's death can be compared with Christ's because by means of it the plan of God enters on its climactic phase. It is the news of John's judicial murder which prompts Jesus to come out of the hidden life and at last to proclaim the Gospel of the Kingdom, the coming of the reign of charity on earth.

SEPTEMBER

1 September, St Gregory the Great

Pope St Gregory never set foot on the soil of this island, and yet he is 'the apostle of the English'. It seems to be a title that goes back to an anonymous Anglo-Saxon biographer, writing in the double monastery founded by St Hilda at Whitby. He calls Gregory I 'our father and apostle in Christ', 'he from whom we have received the Christian faith, he who will present the English people to the Lord on the day of judgment as their teacher and apostle'.

I suppose everyone knows the story of how Gregory was wandering through the Roman forum and saw these very un-Italian looking fair-haired youths being hired as labour, and enquired of what race they were of. 'Angli', he was told, whereupon he replied, 'Non Angli sed angeli', 'Not Angles but angels'. That story does not only tell us that St Gregory appreciated the picturesque. It symbolizes his dawning awareness — and this made him exceptional among the Byzantine civil servants of his day — that a new factor, the Northern peoples, was about to enter the world of Christian civilization.

The two main things to grasp about the apostle of the English are: first, that he was a statesman who saw the need to convert the barbarians at the gates, and as a Christian statesman took that as a missionary challenge; secondly, that he was a monk who wanted to pass onto them with the Gospel the wisdom of the Fathers which laid down the ethical and spiritual foundations for a godly life.

Gregory was not by any means the only bishop interested in christianising the inhabitants of this island. There were others in Gaul and in the Celtic north and west. But by sending Roman missionaries to this country, men with a more refined sense of history, government, culture, Gregory began the process by which the English people came to self-consciousness as a specific nation, *gens Anglorum*, the people of the English.

There's a lot of talk nowadays about an awakening of English (as distinct from British) national feeling or, at any rate, prompted by devolution in the rest of the United Kingdom and anxieties about where the popular culture is heading, a renewed quest for a worthwhile English identity. If our church leaders have half of Gregory's apostolic zeal they can grasp the moment, because, really, you can't make sense of England without the Catholic Church. Let us hope St Gregory is praying for them now.

5 September, Departed Familiars and Benefactors of the Order of Preachers

Today the Order asks us to pray for our departed familiars and benefactors. The term 'benefactor' is understandable enough, but who are these 'familiars'? Clearly, this is not the ordinary English use of the noun which refers to a witch's black cat. Familiars are or were lay people who for various reasons settled in Dominican houses and lived there as lifelong guests but on the understanding that they would contribute to the building up of a given house's life. Normally no money changed hands. Instead they placed some skill or competence at the service of the mission of the Order. In the English Province, the last true familiar, or so I believe, lived at Blackfriars Oxford in the early 1960s. For twenty years, however, from 1980 to 2000, at my own community, Blackfriars Cambridge, we had a stream of lay-people, mostly research students from the University, living in the priory. Three of these, sadly, died tragically young with two of their number, who had married and set up an exemplary household as Catholic academics, leaving little ones behind. We pray for them today.

Benefactors we also have had and have. We remember especially at this Mass Enrichetta and Edward Bullough who gave their dream-house, St Michael's, to the Order in Mrs Bullough's lifetime, having first made the greater sacrifice of giving it both their children. Next we should remember Geoffrey and Daisy Birkbeck who made it possible for us to acquire the other main component of Blackfriars: Howfield, the family home of A. M. Ramsey, sometime Archbishop of Canterbury, and work up the resources to build the connecting section in 1960. Their love for this part of England is reflected in Geoffrey Birkbeck's water colours, of which we have a number of examples scattered through the building.

Many other people have been generous. In the last four years, three widows left us legacies without which we would not have been able to carry out substantial work on the infrastructure of these buildings without devastating our capital holdings. I ought also to mention Canon John Lopes of Fisher House whose estate was disbursed after thirty years of procrastination by his executors. We pray for all of these too.

'Remember me where remembrance is best, at the altar of the Lord': words of St Monica to her son St Augustine. 'Best'. Why? Because here we re-present to the Father the once-for-all Sacrifice of the Son, the Sacrifice offered by the Innocent One for the guilty. The Cross was not only the Sacrifice of One who, as man, was perfectly innocent the 'Lamb without a blemish'. It was the Sacrifice of One who was also God, One whose offering could be taken up by the infinite act of his will as God and so include in its purview all generations, dead, living and yet to be born.

In every celebration of the Holy Eucharist the Church not only worships the Creator and thanks him for his gifts. She also pleads the redeeming Blood. She asks the Father to receive her offering by taking it into Christ's own. She asks for pardon for wrong, enhancement for right, on the basis of the Cross. All is gift or grace but not all is cheap grace. The Crucifix tells us that and the Church's custom of praying for the dead not seventy times but seventy times seven confirms it.

8 September, The Nativity of the Blessed Virgin Mary

Today's feast invites us to consider the birth of our Lady from two angles. The first is from the past, from the angle of the Old Testament. At the Gospel today we read out our Lady's family tree. The Eastern Orthodox sometimes say that the Catholic dogma of her Immaculate Conception cuts Mary off from the ancestors. If there is a totally new start, with no stain of original sin in sight, how can she be in spiritual solidarity with her Israelite forebears? How can she be the Daughter of Zion, summing up all that was best, as well as most distinctive, about the people descended from Abraham, Isaac, and Jacob? This, they say, is false piety which,

while claiming to give Mary a unique 'privilege', actually under-
mines her suitability for her role.

Well, as you heard, we continue to read the genealogy on the
feast of her Nativity despite the dogmatization of the immaculacy
of her origins. And in fact the Immaculate Conception, properly
understood, actually secures what the Orthodox want to say about
her, rather than frustrates it. It was *because* she was filled with grace
from the first moment of her existence that she could take from the
ancestors what was *both* distinctive *and* best for not everything in
the stories of the people mentioned in the family tree was admirable. Not by any manner of means! Not everything there pointed
to human salvation.

And then, secondly, on this feast we look at the Nativity of the
Virgin from a second angle, the angle of the future. This is not just
the birthday of the Virgin. Many people are virgins, there's nothing
so special there. No, this is the Nativity of the *Mother of God*. We
look to what this child will be, this baby girl on whom the Spirit
will descend at the Annunciation to make her the Mother of the
Word himself through whom all things were made. As the Proper
prayers of the Mass put it, she is to be the departure-point of our
salvation.

Not, however, a departure-point like a bus stop when you're
waiting for a coach to take you away somewhere else altogether,
so that the main thing is to leave the departure-point behind. This
is a departure-point that will never be left behind. It's more like
the emergence of a new principle that will inform things ever
afterwards. Mary will be for all ages the woman to whom the Spirit
comes, and the sign of that is: she will always be the woman who
shows us her divine Son.

That is why the greatest of all icons is the divine Child *with his
Mother*, rather than either of them alone.

13 September, St John Chrysostom

John Chrysostom was born into a high-ranking military family and
educated in the schools of Antioch, which were the best for tertiary
education in the fourth century Greco-Roman world. In sharp
contrast to this background he became a monk—indeed, a hermit,

living in a dilapidated cave in the mountains. Despite his entreaties, he was ordained and became a kind of vicar episcopal, with special responsibility for the temporal and spiritual improvement of the condition of the poor.

John's fame as a preacher—his sobriquet 'Chrysostomos', literally 'The Man with the Golden Mouth' attests this—encouraged the East Roman emperor to have him made archbishop of Constantinople in 397, whereupon he launched a decade of moral evangelization. His diversion of wealth to the poor and the health service did not go down well in some quarters, while the disciplinary rules he imposed on the clergy were resented for interfering with freedom of life-style.

His principal opponent was, however, the empress Eudoxia, a kind of combination of Boadicea and Queen Victoria. She took John's drive for moral reform as a personal affront; one of the charges brought against him was treason for allegedly giving her the nickname 'Jezebel'. In 404 he was exiled to somewhere in Anatolia. The forced marches in bad weather brought about his death from exhaustion on 14 September of that year.

St John Chrysostom lived on in ecclesial memory as a new St Paul, someone who revived interest in Paul's teaching and combined it with the mystical theology of the Eastern church: hence his title in the West, one of the four 'Greek Doctors'. In the East that title was, rather, one of the three 'Holy Hierarchs and Universal Teachers'. In other words, it was the Gospel, the apostolic preaching, coming alive again with power, and profiting from the unfolding of its contents in theology and worship.

14 September, The Exaltation of the Holy Cross (1)

Today is the feast of the Exaltation or Triumph of the Holy Cross. On this feast we are celebrating the wood of the Cross as representing the One who suffered and died on it. A day set aside to honour the piece of wood on which Jesus died depends for its sense on what we hold to be true about the meaning of the first Good Friday.

As we know, it is the faith of the Church that on the first Good Friday someone who was God suffered and died as man. Someone freely made the sacrifice of their life, with all the repugnance to natural human instinct which that involves, and that someone was one being with the Creator of the world. The Son of God died as man to demonstrate God's love for us—a love which we could not know about otherwise, just by looking at the world around us. Whatever year you were born in, A. D. 30 is the only year that tells you what your life means.

And there is more. When the Son of God died as man he died not only to tell people in actions that speak louder than words of the Father's love for them as persons, as his individual creations. His sacrifice was also for the sake of changing the whole relationship between God and the world. He merited on behalf of the human race a pardon which human beings, the perpetrators of so many evils, could never have earned, and on that basis the divine life was released in a new way into the world, to permeate history and bring our species to grace and glory. That is what it's all about, what our religion is all about, and why we should never tire of hearing about the Cross of the Lord.

If, then, we share the faith of the Church, we regard the Crucifixion as the central event of world history, and the Cross itself, the physical wood of the Cross, as the instrument and sign of our own ultimate happiness. To make this truth come home to us, to make it sink into us, the Church encourages devotion to the Cross: the making of the Sign of the Cross, for instance. From early times, the faithful built the outline of its shape into the walls of their homes, engraved it on stones and metal carried on their persons. Such devotion was greatly increased by the claim made in the Jerusalem church that the original Cross has been re-located, on September 13th or 14th of a year somewhere between 325 and 334 (at this stage historians can't be more accurate than that), its authenticity verified by the miraculous recovery of a dying man to whom it was applied.

Unless we are deists and deny God's capacity to intervene directly in his own world, we can't rule out the possibility that in this way God *did* return the glorious Cross to the care of the disciples of his Son. At various places in the universal Church tiny pieces of this Cross will be venerated today. (A fragment given to the Bullough family who built St Michael's Cambridge in the mid 1930s is before me in this chapel as I speak.)

But even more important, as we gather for this feast at the Eucharistic altar, is the fact that in the Mass we have among us not the glorious Cross of our salvation but the glorious crucified Saviour himself. In the transformation of the bread and wine into the Lord's Body and Blood into, that is, his real Presence he lives among us still, bearing the marks of his wounds, though now glorified, asking us to unite ourselves with him as he stands before the Father, in praise of the Father, and in that place where he is, which is at once beyond all places and yet gives all places their meaning, he pours out the Holy Spirit by intercession for the world.

14 September, The Exaltation of the Holy Cross (2)

Some of the truths of our religion are so stupendous that we can't take them in at one go. What happened on the Cross is an example of that. On Good Friday we are so concerned with the darkness that the Cross discloses, the depth of humanity's guilt, the extent and range of human sin which was such that only One who was himself the holy God could redeem it, that we don't do justice to the refulgence, the glory, of the Cross. The radiance, joy, triumph of Easter time we fairly naturally associate not with Good Friday but with Easter Day itself or, at the earliest, the Easter Vigil. I'm not saying that we don't spot any inter-connexions between the two. As the celebrant says in marking the Paschal Candle with five incisions for the five wounds of Christ, it is by his holy and glorious wounds that we call on the risen Lord to save us. Still, it's hardly to be gainsaid that the atmosphere of Good Friday is sombre, stripped like the altar, whereas that of Easter is jubilant, smothered in flowers: and this is reasonable, because the Church wants us to register both the depths to which the love of God sank in pursuit of us (Good Friday), and the amazingness of what God did with Christ's atoning work in making it the means by which our human nature now sits at his right hand in glory (Easter Day).

And yet the contrast can make us forget—and here is where today's festival enters the picture—that the Cross is already glorious. Easter is not the reversal of Good Friday. It is not its cancellation, its annulment. On the contrary, Easter is the manifestation, the palpable demonstration, of the content of the Cross. On the Cross, Jesus' sufferings and death reveal the supreme love of God, and it is by his love, the love that God as the Blessed Trinity from all eternity is, with each divine person ceaselessly giving himself away to the others, that God is beautiful.

On the Cross this beauty of the Holy Trinity stoops down to enfold the world in itself, and so what was happening on Good Friday is revealed at Easter in all its power and glory.

And this is why it is so useful to have left behind in the course of history a tangible reminder of the Tree on which all this hung out. Included in today's feast is thanksgiving to God for the discovery in Jerusalem by St Helena, the mother of the first Christian emperor, Constantine, some time around this day, of the remains of the cross-stake on which the Lord had died. Even if it is, surely, quite feasible that early Christians had made a precise note of the site of Calvary, this was a long shot. And yet it fits with everything we know of the plan of God, of how he wanted to manifest his love in the midst of this world's history, of time and of space, that it was in his Providence to keep in the Church's possession the actual pieces of wood on which the Crucified suffered for us.

The splendour of the Cross, its Exaltation, is not just an idea, a theme, or a thesis in theology. It was on this particular bit of hard wood, with these nails and no other, that the flesh of the incarnate Word was secured to the Tree, in order that from there Love in person might reign forever.

15 September, Our Lady of Sorrows (1)

Devotion to our Lady is sometimes regarded as fostering a sentimental view of women, as passive creatures who stay humbly in the background while all the important decisions are made by men. Feminists frequently attack the *cultus* of our Lady which, they claim, portrays her and therefore woman of whom she is the ideal representative—as exclusively soft and receptive, over against a Christ who is firm and active.

Yet the Litany of our Lady calls on her twice in imagery that is certainly firm, not to say military, in character. I'm thinking of the invocations *turris davidica*, 'tower of David', and *turris eburnea*, 'tower of ivory'. These phrases come from the Hebrew Bible, from the Song of Songs, where the bridegroom in the course of praising the bride mentions

> thy neck rising proudly, nobly adorned, like David's embattled tower, thy neck rising proudly like a tower, but all of ivory.

It was a mediaeval theologian, the Frenchman Honorius of Autun, who first used these poetic phrases to speak of Mary. Why? In our own island, Blessed John Henry Newman offered an explanation. In his words:

> A tower is a fabric which rises higher and more conspicuous than other objects in its neighbourhood... It is expressly noted of Mary that she *stood* by the Cross. She did not grovel in the dust, but *stood upright* to receive the blows, the stabs, which the long passion of her Son inflicted upon her every moment.

Mary is, for Newman, rightly imaged as a tower, owing to her strength and courage which compare favourably with the weakness of Peter and the other apostles.

Naturally, this does not mean that our Lady did not have as well the other qualities we classically associate with the feminine. Despite the attempt of radical feminists to turn women into men, the Church will continue to proclaim these softer virtues and glories of Mary also. As Newman (again) puts it:

> She is called the tower *of ivory* to suggest to us, by the brightness, purity, and exquisiteness of that material, how transcendent is the loveliness and the gentleness of the Mother of God.

15 September, Our Lady of Sorrows (2)

At the Cross, there were various ways in which people could be present. The bad thief refused to go beyond mere physical proximity. The good thief turned spatial closeness into a more personal being-with Jesus and was told he would therefore be with him in Paradise that very day. The bystanders, as their name suggests, stood by the Cross with the curiosity of gawpers at a public spectacle. Mary stood by the Cross in a much more significant fashion, consenting to share the destiny of her Son, so that the Father's plan might come to its completion.

By locating the feast of Our Lady of Sorrows so immediately after Holy Cross Day, which fell yesterday, the Church makes it plain that this standing by Jesus at the Cross is the sorrow of Mary *par excellence*. Traditional devotion finds seven such sorrows in the Gospel (seven being the number of fullness) but none is to be put on the same level with this.

The word 'sorrow' is, though, ambiguous. It may just mean the troubles that come to us, even if these are only things permitted by God rather than actually willed by him, and irrespective of their significance or lack of it. Down the ages people have found consolation in the thought that, in a simple, almost naïve, sense of the word 'sorrow', the Mother of Christ shared their typically human sorrows which often, as Shakespeare remarks, come 'not single spies but in battalions'. One of the things that mediaeval Christians relished in the cult of Our Lady of Pity, or in the presence of the Virgin on the Rood which stood above the entrance to the chancels of their parish churches, was Mary's 'kindness' literally, her kinship, her closeness to her kind, humankind, who also, like her, have to bear all sorts of troubles.

But, as we know, the Church has seen in the sorrow of Mary more than that. Our Lady's role in the Sacrifice of her Son is not just more intimate than that of other people standing by: more intimate even than that of St John, the Beloved Disciple. It is also of continuing significance for the transmission of the grace of his Sacrifice through time.

On the Cross Christ died for the Church. He gave himself up for her, so the Letter to the Ephesians tells us, so that she might be his holy Bride without spot or wrinkle or any such thing. Though only the Son of God could make atonement for us, he wanted us to be from the outset included in his Sacrifice. He did not want his Church just to ratify subsequently his once-for-all offering, but to consent to it while it was still proceeding, to give there and then the nuptial consent of the spotless Bride. And this could happen because the Church *was* there, in Mary who is all-responsiveness to the Word.

The sorrow of our Lady that we celebrate today is, then, a redemptive kind of sorrow, since, as Mother of the Church, our Lady has a role in communicating to all generations of the disciples Jesus loves the atoning grace of her Son. The tears of Mary (on which the Gospels are silent but which the poets of Christendom have been unable to believe did not fall at the Cross) do not add to the total of the world's misery, as other tears do. These are the tears — consenting, interceding of Mary's motherly mediation — of the Cross's power, and so wherever they fall, they heal, they ennoble, they purify.

16 September, St Cornelius and St Cyprian

We celebrate today two martyr bishops, who were contemporaries: a pope who died in enforced exile in 253 and a bishop in what is now Tunisia, executed in his episcopal city a few years later.

In the Latin church St Cyprian has sometimes been regarded as the ideal martyr owing to his reluctance to court martyrdom. It was almost too obvious to Christians in the ancient Church that the typical Christian was a martyr. Baptism in water points towards Baptism in blood; Confirmation-commissioning points towards making the final testimony; Eucharistic participation points towards acting out in one's own life the Sacrifice whose fruits one receives in Holy Communion. The most obvious form of the imitation of Christ is to lay down one's life for one's friends. But Cyprian did not favour a policy of deliberately exasperating the authorities so as to make such martyrdom more likely. He fled to the outer suburbs of Carthage, and governed his community by letter from a concealed address. Yet when in the end they caught up with him and the order of arrest was read, he replied, *Deo gratias*. 'Thanks be to God.'

In the martyrs there is a mode of presence of the Christ who entered his glory along the path the martyrs tread. The death of the martyrs is a sacrifice within the single Sacrifice of Christ. In the martyr Christ continues to make fruitful the Sacrifice which he completed on the Cross once and for all.

17 September, St Robert Bellarmine

Today's saint, Robert Bellarmine, reminds us that the Counter-Reformation was less predictable and more sympathetic than is sometimes supposed.

He was born in 1542 in Montepulciano in Tuscany, a very beautiful place. As a young Jesuit, he taught classics, but after ordination at Ghent he became a professor at Louvain (both in present day Belgium) where he read omnivorously and with an extraordinarily retentive memory. When, after his call back to Italy so as to teach in the Roman College, he wrote his massive apologia for the faith, *The Disputations and Controversies*, he was widely believed to be not an individual but a team of scholars: a compliment, of course, to the comprehensiveness and thoroughness of that work. In 1598 Robert was made a cardinal but continued to lead an extremely simple life, dining off bread and garlic and on one occasion pulling down the curtains of his apartment to make do-it-yourself clothing for the poor.

Though in later times he became regarded as the typical Counter-Reformation zealot (copies of his great tome were banned from circulation under English law), he was in fact a moderate of the period: not keen on the notion of the pope's putative authority to depose Christian sovereigns, and a supporter of Galileo. St Robert died on 17 September 1621. He prayed daily by name for King James I and VI of Great Britain and for other Anglican theologians with whom he had entered into debate. Let us hope he also prays for England now.

18 September, St John Macias

St John Macias, born in Spain in 1585, an unlettered boy who tended sheep, had a vision of the apostle John which set him off on his religious career. He crossed the ocean to Spanish America (presumably this was pretty common in an age of settlement of Spaniards on the newly conquered Continent). Initially he resumed his old life as a herdsman, but this time in the Andes. That must have been a matter of waiting to discover an appropriate niche, however, for soon we find him as the porter of the Dominican priory in Lima.

It was a time of extraordinary spiritual renaissance in the vice-regal city: St Rose of Lima was in her hermitage, and St Martin de Porres in a priory with John. The archbishop of Lima of these years was also, incidentally, a canonized saint.

John Macias does not, however, sound like a typical Dominican saint or *beatus* if one has in mind the general identikit picture of an intellectual churchman. All his life he had extraordinary mystical experiences of Christ, our Lady, and St John the Divine. He also experienced spiritual warfare with Satan in a fashion reminiscent of the film *The Exorcist*. He served several Masses each morning, and spent his leisure hours motionless before the Blessed Sacrament. Every night he recited the full Rosary three times for the Holy Souls in Purgatory some of whom appeared to him to seek his intercession. He also had organizational gifts of the kind rarely associated with theologians: preparing and serving food to two hundred of the poor each day, and distributing clothes and medicine by donkey.

It is, however, striking how few of the Dominican saints and *beati* represent an ideal of holiness corresponding to the official aims of the Order in its primary, priestly manifestation. The Order of Preachers is a clerical Order, and yet most of those it has asked Church authority to raise to the altars are not intellectuals, not theologians, not holders of any public office in the Church, and not indeed in any obvious sense apostolic or missionary. Unlettered lay-brothers like John Macias, enclosed nuns, solitaries: these form a high proportion of the total.

Why is this? Perhaps because priests with an apostolate directed above all to the mind, to utilizing the resources of refined intelligence, need those who, as it were, incarnate the spirit of the original Gospel: simple, childlike people, content to sit at the feet of the Saviour, listening to and enjoying his words.

21 September, St Matthew

Hardly anything is known about St Matthew apart from what the Gospels tell us. The martyrologies disagree about where he carried out his mission and met his death. Some say Ethiopia, others Persia. Perhaps they simply mean 'a very long way away', like when we refer to Timbuctoo. In art, his emblems are just inferences from the Gospels: a money-box with a slot in it, a pair of spectacles to help him read his accounts.

So we can say that St Matthew has *become* his Gospel. He entered into the book he made and left no other record in the public life of the Church.

What are *we doing* that the gifts of grace to us may not be in vain? An apostle who became a book is a bit of a reproach to us in this respect. We are often taken up with our own personalities. We forget that we exist just as much in our work.

St Matthew reminds us how important our work for the Church can be in sustaining the Body of Christ in ways we cannot predict. Including there the work that is the *opus Dei*, the 'work of God' that is prayer.

23 September, St Pius of Pietrelcina

Francesco Forgione was born in 1887 into a family of south Italian shepherds, and brought up in an atmosphere of great piety. At the age of five, when in church, he heard a voice which seemed to come from the Eucharistic tabernacle. What it said was, 'You will be scourged and crucified for love of men, but you will bring back many souls into my flock'. When he was fifteen he made vows as a Capuchin friar, taking the name 'Pius' in honour of the Dominican pope Pius V. Fra Pio, though tubercoloid, was much given to severe fasts and penances. His health suffered, which is why he was sent in 1916 to a small and undemanding rural friary, San Giovanni Rotondo, in the hope that he would recover his strength. It can hardly have been expected that he would emerge from it only two or three times before his death in 1968.

This cloistered life carried on in the years to come not for the sake of his health but owing to alarm about the extraordinary phenomena that centred on his person. They came to a climax in two experiences in 1918. The first was 'transverberation'. As classically described by St John of the Cross, this is when 'the soul, being [in John's words] inflamed with the love of God, is interiorly attacked by a seraph who pierces it with a flaming dart', causing intense suffering from the sheer abundance of divine love. The second was when Pius received the stigmata, something that caused him enormous embarrassment. Owing to his ecstasies, the Mass he celebrated regularly took between two and four hours. He spent some fifteen hours a day in the confessional where, like St John Vianney before him, he had gifts of preternatural knowledge. His bilocations, levitations and the miracles he worked read like the more colourful passages in Butler's *Lives of the Saints* (before bowdlerisation by twentieth-century scholars).

The Church understands the stigmata, when authentic, as, along with other physical phenomena of mysticism, a sign of credibility in the given mission of some holy person to the Church and the world. On his death-bed, Pius' stigmata, which had been deep wounds that never formed scabs nor ulcerated but gave off a discernible perfume, are said to have disappeared. It was a sign that his mission was coming to an end. What had his mission been? Surely it was the mission of St Pius of Pietrelcina to bear witness to supernatural realism in a period of scepticism in Western culture, in an age of doctrinal reductionism in the Church. His intercession remains equally needed so long as this period lasts.

24 September, Our Lady of Walsingham

The feast of Our Lady of Walsingham is essentially a celebration of the Incarnation. But it is the Incarnation as earthed in England. Walsingham is, as they say, 'England's Nazareth'. At the heart of it was and is, re-rebuilt under Anglican auspices, the 'Holy House', a symbolic replica of the house of Nazareth. It's not primarily the dwelling of the Holy Family after the return from Egypt that we're talking about here. Mainly, it's the house where Mary was visited by the Lord's angel with the news that she had been chosen to be Mother of the Messiah. That's why the typical Gospel text one hears on visits to Walsingham is the Gospel of the Annunciation.

It was around the time of the Norman Conquest that a Norfolk noblewoman, the Lady Richeldis, had a vision in which the Mother of God asked her to build on East Anglian soil a copy of the house of Nazareth. The idea behind it was obvious. It was to root in that soil the memory of the Incarnation which, later in the mediaeval period, the entire Latin Church fostered in the thrice-daily devotion of the 'Angelus', the prayer that begins, precisely, 'The Angel of the Lord declared unto Mary'. Walsingham is the Angelus turned by anticipation into wood and later brick and flint for the sake of that effective remembering of the greatest News ever brought, that God was to become man. Walsingham is that remembering specifically for England.

It was the love and generosity lavished on this place by our pre-Reformation forebears, not least by the kings of England who came on pilgrimage to Our Lady of Walsingham, that spelt its downfall when greedy heretics cast longing eyes on the riches of the shrine. And it was through the love and generosity of a Catholic laywoman, Charlotte Boyd, and an Anglican parson, Alfred Hope-Patten, that in the first half of the twentieth century England's Nazareth was restored. They gave it two main foci: the Slipper Chapel where pilgrims removed their shoes to walk barefoot the last 'holy mile' to the shrine proper, and the Holy House, with the principal statue of Mary, robed and crowned (except in the penitential seasons), where prayer was found to be more than usually valid and a stream of 'favours' recorded by those who prayed.

What do people pray for at Walsingham? Personal need and private anxiety no doubt make for an endless list, but we are encouraged to pray especially for the Conversion of England, the restoration of the sick, consolation for the afflicted, the repentance of sinners and peace for the departed.

All these are fruits of charity, and the greatest charity the world has ever known was embarked upon in the original house of Nazareth, when the philanthropy of God brought our Maker into Mary's womb.

27 September, St Vincent de Paul

St Vincent de Paul was the kind of cleric we need more off. In the words of Rudyard Kipling, he 'walked with kings but kept the common touch'.

He was tutor to French princes, and pursued a successful apostolate among the rich and powerful, while also specializing in the pastoral care of galley-slaves and convicts. If by their fruits you shall know them, then we do know his mettle. In 1625 he founded the Congregation of the Mission: diocesan priests who would live from a common fund, renounce all ecclesiastical preferment and devote themselves to the needs of the faithful in the smaller towns and villages, all designed to make possible a flexible apostolic life among the secular clergy. He lived to see them spread from the Hebrides to Madagascar. And in 1633 he founded the Sisters of Charity, the first Congregation of unenclosed women, to work among the sick poor.

Entirely appropriately, Pope Leo XIII, faced with the spread of social dislocation through the Industrial Revolution, picked out St Vincent to be the patron of all charitable societies in the Church, of which perhaps the most widespread is the Society of St Vincent de Paul founded in imitation of his example in 1833.

Global recessions come and go. The Lord tells us in the Gospel that the poor we shall always have with us. We should ask for a double share of his spirit for the Church in the world.

29 September, St Michael and all Archangels (1)

Some years ago I celebrated the Mass of the Archangels in a monastic church in the United States which had enjoyed the doubtful privilege of 're-ordering' by a modernizing firm of ecclesiastical architects in the 1970s. The loan of a commemorative brochure about the monastery enabled me to compare 'before' and 'after'. The frescoes of the life of Christ had been whitewashed over; the Stations of the Cross which at any rate had real paint on them had been replaced by toffee-coloured pastel smudges; the delicate rosewood staircase leading to a throne for the highly wrought silver monstrance had been dismantled and the Host was now ensconced in a large stainless-steel lollipop in the middle of the nuns' grille. But most striking of all was the disappearance of the Angels. Around the monstrance (it was a monastery with Perpetual Adoration) they had accompanied the Eucharistic Presence with smoking censers in the vault or stood on guard at intervals down the staircase to the ground. But whether paint or stone one and all had gone, as though they had never been. This set me thinking about what we should lose in the Church if we lost the Angels.

Our first loss would be connected with the sheer scale of the universe we inhabit. Our physical universe, the expanding universe of modern cosmology, is bigger than that of our mediaeval forebears, though the medievals also believed its size to be staggeringly large. But in losing the hosts of heaven, the angelic realms that interpenetrate the universe of matter in traditional Christian thought, we would lose a sense of the multi-dimensional spaciousness of the world we inhabit. The Angels are (I should have thought) particularly needed in enclosed monasteries to remind cloistered nuns that the enclosure, which creates physical confines, is meant to open them to a larger room not a smaller one than the ordinary world experiences.

But then in the second place, losing sight of the Angels we also lose sight of a vital feature of the mission of Christ. When the Word became man he entered the realm not only of matter but also of created spirit and that means not just the realm of human soul and human intelligence but also the realm of the Angels, the angelic intelligences. The words of Jesus to Nathaniel about how henceforth the Angels will ascend and descend on the Son of Man tell us that the activity of the Angels in the human world is now always to be seen with reference to Christ: it proceeds now in strict association with him. In the New Testament, Angels attend the most important moments in the self-manifestation of the Word: the Annunciation, the Passion, the Resurrection and Ascension, and this speaks to us of the way the threshold between the earthly and the heavenly is being thrown open through the God-man.

And thirdly, we need the Angels because, according to the mystical experience of the Church, what the Angels provide is above all spiritual clarity: the light they give our spirits prepares us for the encounter with the uncreated Light of God himself which, were we to see it now, would overwhelm us by its super-radiance. We must open our minds to the Angels on earth so that they may help us open our minds to the Lord in heaven.

Possibly we can think of the Angels in too 'Michaeline' a way: too much as, like St Michael, mighty powers that guard and defend in the cosmic battle between good and evil. But Angels can also be

'Raphaeline', as revealed in St Raphael who carried out such humble, discreet self-effacing tasks in the service of the family of Tobias. To be at our service, including the service of our inner life of will, thought and feeling, murky as it so often is: this is for these spirits a self-humiliation they willingly perform as aid to our salvation.

29 September, St Michael and all Archangels (2)

It wasn't the Dominicans who called this place (Blackfriars Cambridge) 'St Michael's'. It was the Bullough family who built the house of that name and gave it to the Order of Preachers. From the old front door it is possible to see how much the name built to them. The door has a whole frieze cut into the stonework of Michael fighting Satan. And in Professor Bullough's study, what we now call the Old Library, there is an iron relief of the Archangel triumphing over Satan at the back of the fireplace. All the friars have done is add a couple more images of St Michael, in paint or glass, here and there.

Why was Edward Bullough so focussed on this Archangel? Bullough, eventually Serena Professor of Italian in the University of Cambridge, was a fervent convert to Catholicism who was to become the president of Pax Romana, the pontifical organization for liaison among Catholic academics world-wide. He and his wife saw their house as not just a private dwelling but a centre of public Catholicism in Cambridge. Before women undergraduates were admitted to the Catholic Chaplaincy, he took responsibility, as treasurer of the University's Catholic Association, for the social and intellectual life of the Catholics among them. Their soirées and the conferences he arranged for their ongoing formation took place at St Michael's.

All around them, in the respectable groves of academe, a battle was raging. This was the age of Cambridge Communism, of the Cambridge spies. Furthermore, through, not least, the society called (ironically enough!) 'The Apostles', the intellectual leadership of the University had been for years openly or covertly agnostic. For Bullough to call his house 'St Michael's was to make a statement that there was a war on: a spiritual war, but a war nevertheless.

Bullough was a literary man, but he was interested in natural science. He was something of a pioneer in bringing together art appreciation and the scientific study of the process of perception. So he wasn't simply being reactionary when he sought the patronage of the Archangel. For the question is, What is the overall character of the cosmos that science explores? Is the range of that cosmos limited to the material world, which scientific instruments register with the help of mathematics? Or has it many dimensions?

We know from revelation that the latter is the case. In the beginning, God created not only 'the earth', the world that natural science can study, but also (and we notice this is mentioned first in Scripture) 'the heavens', which are another dimension. The prior creation of the heavens means that when the Big Bang or the initial singularity or whatever you wish to call the first moment of matter actually happened, the universe was already conscious. It was expecting us, awaiting us with a benevolence and compassion we shall never fully understand. The Holy Angels, who are sheer minds (and wills) were, as Scripture presents them, utterly immersed in God and yet they were turned towards the world we inhabit.

There is something truly marvellous about the way Scripture depicts the Angels. The Bible includes a revelation of angelic love. Angelic love is the specific variety of sacrificial love by which the angelic realm which is not human and already enjoys the vision of God nevertheless sets itself to serve us and involves itself in struggle for our ultimate wellbeing.

Until we get to heaven, we shall not know all that the Angels have done for us. But as Edward Bullough seems to have surmised, it will probably centre on guarding our minds from evil: minimising the force of ideas that corrode the good, and the capacity of evil to seek and find collusion in our own hearts. That is the battle we are involved with every time we open the daily newspaper or get up in the morning to face a new day with other people.

Today's celebration tells us that when we wake up each day, we are not just waking up to the wallpaper. We are waking up to a world where the sleepless Angels are watching.

30 September, St Jerome

There were times in his ministry when our Lord adopted a denunciatory mode, angered at hardness of heart. Debates with the Pharisees are an obvious example; so also is his excoriation of the three towns of the so-called 'evangelical triangle' (Bethsaida, Capernaum, Chorazin) at the north end of the Sea of Galilee where so much of his preaching was concentrated.

In the Sanctoral Cycle, that might bring to mind today's saint, Jerome of Bethlehem, a doctor of the patristic Church whose biting use of irony and stirring up of controversy was equally unwelcome to *his* contemporaries.

St Jerome is chiefly celebrated for his Scripture scholarship: he is the patron of biblical studies in the Catholic Church. Perhaps it was because his mind was so steeped in Scripture that he reacted as he did to the average Christians of his time. In his sometimes excessive advocacy of the place of the ascetics in the Church Jerome was opposing what in the 1960s would be called 'bourgeois Christianity': the religion of respectable, comfortably off people who thought that with a modicum of good-will and church-going God would be at ease with them as they slipped into heaven.

But the Word of God searches the heart and puts a sharp knife-blade between its fibres. And what it finds in the heart of man has its issue on Calvary. Jerome lacked the virtue of moderation—at any rate, outside his activities as a judicious translator. Yet moderation by itself is a pretty inadequate response to the enormity of human malice and the violent death of One who was God.

OCTOBER

1 October, St Thérèse of the Child Jesus

St Thérèse of the Child Jesus, 'The Little Flower', seems to sum up
the objections of many ordinary people to the lives of cloistered
nuns. It was in every sense a cloistered life. Born towards the end
of the nineteenth century into a devout, somewhat introverted
middle-class family, she was brought up surrounded by practices
and images of piety. Her mother, who died when Thérèse was four,
had only girls, all four of whom entered the Carmel of their local
town, Thérèse herself at the age of fifteen. During her short life
(she died when she was twenty-four), she never did anything
remarkable: certainly nothing that in any tangible way benefited
the human race. When she was dying the members of her sisterhood wondered whatever they could put in her obituary notice
because, even by their standards, which were scarcely exigent, her
life was almost totally uneventful: a wave passing over the sand
and barely leaving an outline behind it.

Within thirty years she was not only canonised but declared
patroness of the missionary outreach of the Church, an outreach
considerably more intense and extended then than now.

What happened in between? The discovery of her autobiography demonstrated how she herself had rediscovered, in the most
dramatic way, the essence of discipleship. Her devotion to the
Child Jesus was combined with what seemed its opposite: a
struggle in darkness with atheism and despair. The result was her
petite voie: the 'little way' of spiritual childhood. That means:
clinging to the hidden God in trust at every moment of one's life.
Her language of flowers, which was sufficiently widespread in
nineteenth and twentieth century French literature to constitute
what one critic has called a 'flower poetic', was not sentimentality,
as we might all too easily think. It was a fulfillment of the biblical
saying, 'Out of the strong comes sweetness'. Her concept and
practice of charity were total: hence no action was too small to be
worth doing as well as possible. No gesture, no word, no inflection

of the voice were too insignificant to become the vehicle of charity. No duty was too routine or humdrum to be the means of excellence.

On her death-bed her confidence was that of one who already, in this life, has gone through Calvary to Easter. Her promise that after her death she would 'shower down roses' has as its background the pious practice of spreading rose-petals in church at Pentecost. At the heart of the Church she had become, quite simply, an agent of the Holy Spirit.

2 October, The Guardian Angels

Though there are indications in Scripture about angel guards, the Church's belief about the Guardian Angels is expressed chiefly in the Liturgy. It is not dogma, but it is doctrine in the sense that what is laid down when we pray is a norm for faith.

Interest in angel guardianship may seem ultra-pious and exclusively ecclesiastical. Yet many of the traditional theologians who have written about it are inclined to present it as something completely natural, with no special relation to the Christian economy or the mystery of the Church. For them, you get your guardian angel at your birth, not at your Baptism.

That way of seeing things fits with the view that angel guardianship is a general dispensation of Providence to keep the human race as wholesome as its fallen circumstances permit. For St Thomas, for example, the most direct and typical effect of the effort of these angels is an access of intellectual light in the human mind. The human species is kept in approximate mental equilibrium through the watchfulness of these spirits. And it is a remarkable thing that, despite the many fatuous or aberrant things that individuals or whole societies can come to believe about life, the human race can be expected to respond to a call back to some fundamental truths and decencies. If this picture is roughly correct it is because of the angel guardians that, say, papal encyclicals addressed to all people of good will have some chance of a hearing.

And yet the Guardian Angels are not concerned with world-historical forces as such but with each of us. It is Thomas again who points out that the secrets of grace are person-to-person. The dealings of the Holy Trinity with us are not en masse but as personal rational creatures. So it's not surprising that individual angels are chosen to watch over individual souls treated with such intimate and delicate care by God himself. This is how the writers of the English Catholic Revival wrote of them. In Newman's 'The Dream of Gerontius', the angel guardian salutes Gerontius, 'My friend and brother, hail!', and in Faber's hymn 'Angels of Jesus', they wait ready to greet the individual pilgrims whose companions each has been:

> Angels of Jesus, angels of light
> singing to welcome the pilgrims of the night.

4 October, St Francis of Assisi

When Dominicans preach on St Francis—our 'holy and seraphic father', as the Dominican liturgical books call him, following their Franciscan equivalents, they quite often poke fun at the sentimental Anglo-Saxon view of the saint. This was a saint who was utterly Christ-centred, absorbed in the mystery of the Passion and Cross (he received the stigmata, for goodness' sake), someone who was unbending about absolute poverty, and whose final testament, far from being a manifesto of an all-appealing Broad Churchmanship, was an almost embarrassing statement of ultra-Papalism. Very different, in other words, from the lovey-dovey St Francis, surrounded by fuzzy toy animals, in late Victorian 'children's corners'. So perhaps it is worth righting the balance and saying how the animal-loving, proto-ecological St Francis is not a myth or an illusion but is well and truly grounded in the sources.

The primitive sources tell us Francis forbade the brethren to cut down whole trees, he insisted on the planting of sweet-smelling flowers in gardens, he picked up worms from the road in case they were crushed, and he ordered that the best wine be set out for the bees in winter time. Among all animals, we are told, he preferred the gentle.

Gentle to whom, we might ask? Still, there is here an extraordinary development of the biblical outlook on the animal world. Admittedly, in the Psalter all kinds of creatures are found praising the Lord, but in the other biblical book where animals are prominent, the Book of Job, gentleness is far from central. What Job is told, in effect, is: look at the animal world in its bizarre and frightening splendour. Look at lion, raven, deer, hawk, vulture, water buffalo, crocodile (all these are specifically mentioned), and realize that both the creation and the Creator are a good deal stranger than Job has appreciated so far.

Yet that is not the whole story. When in Genesis Adam names the animals, and when in Isaiah the prophet foretells the ultimate harmony of all things when the lion will lie down with the lamb, something else—something different, if not necessarily something contradictory—is being said. And what we find in the lives of a number of the saints (Francis is scarcely alone in this) is what we can call a renewal of the original peace of creation by way of foretaste of the peace of the Age to Come. And 'gentleness', the word chosen by the early Franciscan biographers, has a lot to do with this.

'My sisters the swallows' ceasing to chirp at Francis' request so that a sermon could be heard, or 'sister cicada' coming to sing for him by sitting on his hand: these are not everyday experiences. But they are nevertheless an intensification of the collaboration between animals and human beings which we all know in part. A modern biologist has written a book called *Dogs that Know when their Owners are Coming Home and Other Unexplained Powers of Animals*, and there is talk by some of an 'empathosphere' where the mutual sympathy of man and beast creates a sort of ripple-effect spreading out to others of our and their kind.

The good Lord (this was Francis' intuition) has put us into a world that is a 'cosmic friary', where in different senses we are in a condition of brotherhood and sisterhood not just with fellow-Christians or fellow-humans but with a wider fellowship too. And what it all means we shall only discover in the peaceable Kingdom, in the peace of God which at present passes our understanding.

7 October, Our Lady of the Rosary (1)

As we know, the Rosary is a way of meditating on the mysteries of the life of Christ and our Lady's role in those mysteries. So it's a way of contemplating the mystery of salvation itself—first and foremost in the One by whom salvation was accomplished for us, Jesus Christ, and then secondly in her through whom salvation has come to us because she is not only the Mother of the Word Incarnate but the Mother of the Church as well.

That makes the Rosary a highly objective way of praying, because it focuses on the great events in which God was engaged to save us. Yet at the same time it leaves us complete freedom to home in on whatever aspect of each of those events we personally find most moving or inspirational.

That combination of objectivity and freedom is summed up in the symbolic title we give this prayer: the Rose-garden. A garden is landscaped. It has a particular shape and lay-out that is definite and given. But within that landscape you can wander at will.

And that is not the only thing that makes a garden a good place to turn for the name of this prayer. In Scripture, whose authors, unlike the British, were worried by lack of rainfall, the land turning into desert, a garden represents flourishing, happiness, beatitude. So a garden is a good image for salvation, and for a prayer that speaks of salvation. A designed garden tells us about its maker, and it has the effect of protecting the house it surrounds and consoling those who live there. The Gospel of Jesus Christ tells us about its designer, God the Holy Trinity, and his plan for us, and it too is protective and consoling. It is a balm for the scrapes and spills, some of them grave, even mortal, that no human life escapes completely. Yes of course, it's also demanding and challenging. But it's not only that it would be inhuman to expose yourself to demand and challenge all day every day. We also need protection and consolation, and Scripture is full of the divine promise that we are to receive them.

The sacramentals, the blessed roses, which in Dominican churches we give out after Mass today will speak to us of that.

7 October, Our Lady of the Rosary (2)

On the feast of the Rosary we are doing two things. First, we are thanking God for the unique person of the Virgin Mary and that means for her crucial role in the events that founded our religion and changed the direction of the history of the world. By Rosary prayer, we look at those events, the story of Jesus Christ, through the eyes of the Mother of the Church. The Rosary involves meditation (perhaps via just one thought, one insight) on the events that were key in our salvation: what we call 'the mysteries', joyful, sorrowful, glorious, and now also luminous (if we wish to add them, for Pope John Paul II, in introducing them, left that to each person's discretion).

In the Joyful Mysteries, we look along with Mary as the person who gave the Word human birth and nurtured him as he grew up as man. In the Luminous Mysteries, we look along with Mary as she followed, sometimes with anxious questioning, the line of development of the public ministry. In the Sorrowful Mysteries, we look along with her as she stood by the Cross and witnessed his apparent failure and, so far as the world was concerned, his extinction. In the Glorious Mysteries, we look along with her as witness to the new life of the Resurrection: the discovery that his execution was actually the all-fruitful Sacrifice, the results of which are grace and glory for the human race.

But then secondly today we also thank God for the Rosary prayer itself. It's a prayer which, if not disclosed miraculously as some have said, at any rate grew up providentially. It is the people's charter for mystical prayer. It is the poor man's way to mystical prayer, telling us that each of us, whatever our spiritual poverty, can become true contemplatives. The least sophisticated and the most sophisticated can pray the Rosary in different ways. Each can find their prayer life becoming in the best sense simple. More and more, it can consist in just looking at God, concentrating on him as he has revealed himself to us. That in any case is how, according to the faith of the Church, Mary herself now sees him in her bliss.

9 October, Blessed John Henry Newman

How shall we remember this great priest? As pastor and director of souls? As literary luminary, the greatest contributor of anyone in the Catholic Church to modern English prose? As figurehead of the Catholic Revival in England? As patron of the Ordinariate of Our Lady of Walsingham, for Anglicans in communion with the Holy See? Yes, all of this. And yet, without seeking to anticipate some future judgment by the Church, we will surely find him above all *among the holy doctors*. Though not formally numbered among them, they furnish his natural and supernatural setting.

What, then, can he do for us as teacher, as one best approached in the company of the doctors?

In the first place, he can give us a sense of the heights and depth, the length and breadth of revelation. In Newman's eyes, revelation is the immensely generous truth of God, entering the fabric of our minds as a living and comprehensive idea, relevant to all facets of our life—indeed, to all facets of reality—and able by its own vitality to penetrate and transform the entire culture in which, through us, it lives and breathes. Newman holds out to us a vision of how revealed truth is utterly objective and all-engaging. That is why he set his face against what we today would call the privatization of religion. In his speech of thanks to the pope when made a cardinal he described his whole life, both as Anglican and as Catholic, as a struggle against the spirit of liberalism in religion, he meant the notion that religion is private opinion, that the 'Governor of the universe' (as he put it) does not care what views we adopt as ultimate truth.

But in the second place Newman teaches us that the act of faith is a deeply personal act. If we are to give revelation 'real' and not just 'notional' assent, it must come from the heart. 'Heart speaks to heart' was the motto he adopted as his own, and in his sermons and discourses that was what he set out to do: to testify personally, and to persuade by appeal to the hearts of his hearers. Avoiding emotionalism, he knew that truth must reach us at the greatest level of depth of which we are capable, and that will mean at our personal centre, at what the poet Yeats called 'the deep heart's core'. Or else we shall miss holiness of life and without holiness of life Christian truth loses its best possible guard.

Clergy and laity, we must be for Newman as holy as we are well-instructed. And he is right. This is why Blessed John Henry is a teacher whose message we cannot afford to ignore.

13 October, St Edward the Confessor

In many societies, people have difficulty in recognizing as legitimate an authority that is not personal. In countries where the State is weak, or, as in Italy, lacks a continuous history, this is very clear. But even in this country there were occasional reports of women curtseying to Mrs Thatcher. Looked at with the cold eye of social psychology, the institution of kingship corresponds to this need, and its Christianisation is one of the triumphs of the mediaeval Church. The evolution of the Western coronation rites shows how the image was built up of the virtues the good king should have and the principles he should govern by.

In sharp contrast to his pagan Anglo-Saxon predecessors before the Conversion, Edward the Confessor was canonized for his exemplary accessibility to all, his generosity to the poor and his perpetual continence. That may show that St Edward was rightly venerated in his own time, but what about *our* time when monarchy even in England is hardly a major factor in life? Here is where we leave social psychology and enter the realm of theology.

At the pinnacle of things is God in his sovereign greatness. All high office should in some way iconise that greatness in its power yet mercy. The machinery of parliamentary democracy leaves little room for that: it is too workaday. In *The Lord of the Rings* Tolkien realized that kingship is one of the things people universally respond to even if they are, for example, Americans. In modern England we are alternately sentimental and cynical about kingship. One way we could overcome that is by giving St Edward the honour that is his due.

15 October, St Teresa of Avila

St Teresa was born in Spain's heroic age, the end of the fifteenth and the early part of the sixteenth centuries. The Moors thrown back into North Africa, the Americas discovered, it was a new world where the sky was the limit. Her way of being part of it was adventurousness in doing great things for God. She founded dozens of monasteries of the reformed Carmelite Order on journeys when she often slept under the stars. To help her work forward she conducted a correspondence with grandees and high ecclesiastics, and above all with the king, in letters where she is respectful but firm and demanding.

In her relations with God she had the same swashbuckling, all-or-nothing approach, which one might almost call 'dare-devil', and I suppose it did dare the Devil to do his worst to so powerful an exponent of confidence in the grace of God.

It didn't begin easily, which is an encouragement to us. As a young nun, she was subject to inexplicable migraines and palpitations; she describes herself as vain, at the mercy of her emotions, making foolish friendships, and spending her prayer time wishing the clock round. In *The Book of her Life* she explains that it all began to change for her when she really started to love Jesus Christ. 'I started again to love the most Sacred Humanity. Prayer began to take shape as a building that now had a foundation.' And as Jesus counsels in the Gospel, she never looked back.

17 October, St Ignatius of Antioch

'It is better to be silent and be real than to talk and be unreal': words of Ignatius of Antioch, martyred around the year 100 in Rome.

Thanks to his wonderful letters, written to the various churches he encountered, or passed near to, on his journey to execution, Ignatius is undoubtedly one of the most important figures in Christian history in the period immediately following the apostles. But given that quotation I started from, and there are others like it, he is a rather improbable figure for preachers to model themselves on. Preachers spout, whereas St Ignatius had a very high doctrine of silence.

The eternal Word of God, he says, issues from the silence of the Father. The silence of God is not a sterile, dead silence, but is filled with generativity, with spiritual life. So, Ignatius writes, the bishop, the head of each local church, must reflect the Father by his own silence. And this is not just for bishops. The person who really grasps the words of Jesus Christ is, he adds, the person who can hear Jesus' silence.

He means by that, you have to be sensitive to what is tacit, implicit, in Jesus' words, the total context from out of which they come. That includes, and most importantly, the fact that as the Word incarnate Jesus comes out of the silence of the Father.

This does not necessarily contradict, however, a high doctrine of preaching. An inscription sometimes seen in Dominican cloisters reads, *Silentium pater praedicatorum*: 'Silence is the father of preachers'. If study is to be contemplative and generate insight into Christian truth, large areas of silence are needed so as to let things sink in and start to form connexions with one another and ultimately with God. Silence is a prerequisite of apostolically fruitful study, and this is not surprising if study is bound up with contemplation: silence, so long as it is really desired, for the right reasons, and not just grudgingly tolerated, generates a contemplative atmosphere.

I think St Ignatius would have known what I'm talking about.

18 October, St Luke

We owe to St Luke not only his Gospel-book but also the Acts of the Apostles which is the second volume of a two part work, and shows how the Gospel message, along with its vehicle, the Church, spread out from Palestine into the wide world.

Early tradition attests that Luke was from cosmopolitan Antioch, a Gentile by origin, a medical doctor by profession and an artist by inclination. Nothing contrary to those claims emerges from modern scholarship.

The mediaeval Italian poet Dante called St Luke the 'scribe of the gentleness of Christ', and this is accurate. Only Luke records such parables of our Lord's compassion as the Good Samaritan and the Prodigal Son; only he gives us the words of Christ on Calvary to the Good Thief and, on the Way of the Cross, the address to the Women of Jerusalem, both of which in their different ways are expressions of care and concern.

More widely, his Gospel-book is very women-oriented. He has a rich theology of our Lady and, in general, female figures play a bigger part than with the other evangelists. But he is not sentimental: he stresses a combination of poverty, prayer and purity of heart reflecting the best of Old Testament piety as well as Jesus' own teaching and example.

In his prologue, he tells the dedicatee how he sought out all the eye-witness testimony he could. It is more than doubtful whether he shared the belief of some radical exegetes today that the various New Testament communities barely knew each other and had quite different Gospel-messages to offer. Like the most fruitful contributions to catholicity, Luke is distinctive without being dissenting.

28 October, St Simon and St Jude

So far as this world knows, today's saints came together for the last time when their relics were translated to Rome, where they are housed in the Basilica of the Twelve Apostles which was once the parish church of the Old Pretender, otherwise King James III and VIII. Before that, the tradition of the West links them in their post-Pentecost lifetimes as preaching in Persia; the tradition of the East says Syria. We celebrate them today as both apostles and martyrs.

The Church always assumes an apostle to be a martyr unless there is some compelling reason for thinking otherwise. This assumed connexion between being and apostle and being a martyr derives from an insight into the nature of apostolic tradition.

The original 'tradition' was not only Jesus' instruction of the disciples as professional rememberers, trained up to hand down by oral tradition his words and actions. It was also the divine act of 'handing over' (the same word, whether in Greek or Latin) by which the Father gave up his only Son to the death which saved the world. The apostles taught what Jesus had taught, together with the meaning of the Paschal Mystery. Those of them who were also evangelists took exactly that format for their Gospel-books.

So, for the apostles, faithfulness to the reproduction of Christ's teaching—and this is orthodoxy—was inseparable from witness to the meaning of his Paschal Mystery, and such witness cannot be given without a sacrificial approach to living and dying and this is orthopraxy. Orthodoxy and orthopraxy go together since both belong equally to tradition.

The Church is founded on that faithful witness of the apostles. In that unsurpassable moment of foundation, St Simon and St Jude played their parts.

NOVEMBER

1 November, Solemnity of All Saints (1)

As a Lancastrian, it pains me to say it, but today's Solemnity is almost certainly a gift of Yorkshire to the Catholic Church. Our first clear evidence for it comes from around the year 700 at York Minster, and in the following century it was taken to the Frankish empire by Alcuin of York who became Charlemagne's librarian. There are two homilies for the feast ascribed to the Venerable Bede, and though modern scholars may reject this traditional ascription, at least they agree that it points us in the right direction: to the area where Roman Christianity met the Celtic Church in the north-east of England. Ancient Celtic, especially Irish, Christians loved litanies: simple prayers arranged in great long lists, and these litanies could include not only address to individual saints but invocations of whole categories of saints: prophets and patriarchs, apostles and martyrs, virgins and confessors. Probably that is where devotion to 'all the saints' started — in the Irish 'breastplate' prayers where people sought the protection of huge swathes of the population of heaven.

That is the background history of All Saints. But what is the use of this feast? What does it mean?

What it means is the inseparable unity of our destiny *in* God but *with* other people. It is a celebration of the social character of heaven. A modern author has defined human beings as 'rational dependent animals'. It's our being rational that tells us our destiny can only be in God. It's because we have a restless desire to understand, a desire to which no limits can be set (as the advance of modern science testifies) that our final destiny can only be in God. Only God is great enough to be a reality fit for us in the last analysis, to spend our lives—it might be better to say our 'existence'—knowing. Only he is inexhaustible enough to satisfy the inexhaustibility of our own minds.

But we are not only rational, we are according to the definition I gave you rational *and dependent*: dependent not least on each other, dependent on each other in a whole variety of ways. That includes: for complementary insights of mind and heart, for diversion, for companionship, and ultimately, for communion for just enjoying the co-existence of others with ourselves. The vision of God cannot exclude that or it would satisfy one side of our nature, the rational side, while denying another side, the dependent side. The vision of God must have then a social dimension.

And finally, we are not just rational and dependent, we are rational dependent *animals*. That we are animals, who live in the body and are meant to, tells us that the fulfillment of our desire to understand in God, in dependence on other people—the social joy of heaven—can't come about without some major change to the world. Simply surviving death as souls with an immortal aspect to them won't get us social embodied life in God as, precisely, transfigured animals. That, of course, is what the Incarnation of God, the Word of God's descent into our flesh, and his own Death, Resurrection and Ascension in our flesh, taking our human nature with him to God, was all about.

1 November, Solemnity of All Saints (2)

On the feast of All Saints we celebrate heaven. So what is heaven? The 'Penny Catechism' answers obliquely by saying why heaven is worth celebrating: 'The glory and happiness of heaven is to love, see and enjoy God for ever'. The 1992 *Catechism of the Catholic Church,* rather more directly, calls heaven 'this mystery of blessed communion with God and with all who are in Christ' and the latter part of that reply shows why heaven is celebrated as, more specifically, the feast of all the saints.

Whichever of the two statements one prefers, either is preferable to some of the proposals floated when I was in my student years, in the later 1960s and 70s. In that period, we might well have been offered some version of transcendental sociology or, alternatively, mystical biology.

Perhaps, it was suggested, heaven is the 'definitive humanization of the structures of society'. Or again, while heaven might not be attainable on this planet which, after all, could become uninhabitable before we reach that happy condition, perhaps the human species will go on transforming itself while moving from one planetary habitat to another. Isn't it possible that, given the right sort of politics and the best possible technology, the human race could be perfectible and, for all practical purposes, immortal, and all this without ever invoking God and the supernatural?

It's hardly necessary, I think, to follow up such speculations for the simple reason that there is *no such person as the human race*. It is persons alone who are actual: real subjects of a life, true agents in human living. And it's the frustration and waste in the lives of persons that creates the moral necessity for heaven. 'Heaven' is our necessary word for all that lies beyond human experience as the fulfillment which that experience postulates in the light of the goodness of God revealed in Jesus Christ.

St John of the Cross remarks in one of his maxims, 'It is on love we shall be judged in the evening of our days'. I am sure he is talking about love like that of our Redeemer, which excludes whatever is indulgent and self-regarding, and includes whatever is sacrificial and generous. And in the light of Jesus Christ precisely that is what we can take forward into the night of death. *That* is what will be taken forward into heaven. That is what will survive in the presence of God. And it is how we shall be fulfilled. The triumph of love is the way the tears of all who suffer now will be wiped away. That is why the central image of heaven, as the last book of Scripture presents it, is the Lamb of sacrifice surrounded by his saints.

We speak of Christ's intercession for us with the Father, and of the prayers of the saints which he presents to the Father on our behalf. So we can on this feast go further, and say: even now, heaven is not apart from earth. Heaven is actively engaged on earth, drawing earthly persons into its own fulness, its own marvellous radiance.

2 November, All Souls' Day (1)

Today's celebration reminds us that the Church has never reconciled herself to the fact of death as we know it. Death is the internal destruction of the body-soul unity of man. It is also the external destruction of friendship and relationship.

Like St Paul, the Church sees death as we know it as the result of a terrible breakdown in the plan of God: 'sin entered the world, and with sin, death'. In this the apostle was in tune with his Master who wept at the grave of Lazarus his friend, and cried into the darkness of the tomb, 'Lazarus, come forth'.

Unreconciled to the fact of separation, we call out across the barrier of death, especially at this time of year, the season when nature herself is entering her yearly grave. We call out above all to our fellow-Christians. We do not only pray to the saints, as on yesterday's Solemnity, we also pray to the 'holy souls', those who like us are still being redeemed, but in Purgatory. And we remind ourselves that we also must cross this dreadful threshold. 'Pray for us now and at the hour of our death.'

The younger we are, the less we tend to have any experience of bereavement, while by contrast the elderly often feel themselves to be simply survivors of the dead. But perhaps one could say that the less experience we have in this domain, the more important it is to maintain a sense of the great seriousness of dying. A grizzled old bed-ridden lady I once took communion to in a town in the central old industrial belt of Scotland said to me, 'The Catholic religion is a hard one to live in, but an easy one to die in.' But we have to beware of turning that formula upside down, and leaving people unprepared for death without a scenario, or a spiritual geography for the realm of death such as the Catholic doctrine of Purgatory has provided.

We have to resist a tendency to sentimentalise death, to canonize all the departed faithful and unfaithful and every gradation in between, to turn the Requiem Mass from a sacrifice of expiation for the dead into a service of thoughtful remembrance of them. We have to resist that not just in the name of orthodoxy but also, I think, of simple human reality. The single most important function religion plays in people's lives is to enable them to face their own deaths and the deaths of others; to turn the energy of grief to good spiritual use, in an offering of charity, to help the dead to be purified for the vision of God.

And as with everything in our religion, it all comes down ultimately to Jesus Christ. It's because he is so completely the 'only Mediator' between God and man that he can freely make us in our turn into mediators of him, can take our prayers and sacrifices into his own self-offering to the Father and make them fruitful for the life everlasting.

2 November, All Souls' Day (2)

Probably how we approach All Souls' Day depends very much on whether we have ever known grief, itself well described as the price one pays for love. If we have never wept for someone, even with dry tears, we may well not feel the instinctive urge to pray for the dead. Conversely if we have so wept, then, unless our minds are cluttered up with the wrong sort of theology, nothing is more instinctively normal than to pray for the dead.

Praying is all we can do for the dead. The time for anything else is past. This, however, we can still do. It's something of a mystery why the churches born in the Protestant Reformation rejected this urge as something that could not be brought into relation with the saving grace of Christ. As St Thomas More put it, 'I cannot bethink me how any Christian man could find it in his own conscience to search out reasons why other Christian men should not pray for their fellows'. No matter how many memorial services or thanksgiving services there may be for the life of X or Y, there is no substitute for the act of beseeching heaven for the soul of one you love.

It was in that spontaneous way that the ancient Church began to pray for her dead members as well as for the living. The first signs are popular inscriptions, graffiti scratched on the walls of the catacombs and suchlike places where early Christians buried their dead. 'Give peace to Marius'; 'Peace be to you, Cecilia'. Nobody had theories about it. It was the pure language of Christian faith, hope and charity. Christ the Lord had risen from the dead, and in the radiant light of Easter all life was to be seen in relation to the victorious Lord of life. He is the one who showed that the living God is stronger than death.

If Christ has been made in his glorious Resurrection the Source of new life for us, then the decisive thing is to be near the Source. Biology, the science of life, becomes Christology, the science of Christ. Biological life is possible in the last analysis because it is the gift of the all-creative Word of God, One through whom all things were made. Those who had been in a personal relation with him as their Redeemer, through faith and the sacraments of faith, would hardly be put beyond his powers by undergoing death.

Indeed not, which is why our central act of prayer for the dead is the offering of the Mass, where we can weave our own poor scraps of prayer into the mighty prayer of Christ himself before the Father. We are here to plead before his Throne of grace.

3 November, St Martin de Porres

Shrines erected to St Martin de Porres, complete with monthly magazines where supernatural 'favours received' are advertised, are quite a common phenomenon in the popular Catholicism of various parts of the world including our sister island across the Irish Sea. Many people are tempted to be snooty about this sort of thing. Yet if we look at the ancient historian Peter Brown's study of the rise of the cult of the saints in early Christianity we find it fits perfectly well into the patristic landscape, into the world of the Fathers of the Church.

Brown argues that historians have written off the cult of the saints as the invasion, by superstitious masses, of what was otherwise, in the time of such Church Fathers as St Augustine, a rather satisfactory elite religion: monotheistic, coherent and even rational. But, says Brown, none of the intellectual heavyweights of the age of the Fathers ever distanced themselves from these so-called 'popular' beliefs, though they occasionally objected to the privatization of the veneration of the saints when local communities or families cut off access to the saint by the wider Church, the common mother. That, surely, was a compliment to the cult of the saints, not a criticism of it.

What the cult of the saints did was to break down the sense of barriers between heaven and earth. It combined divine power with intimate human presences, and so changed the perception of what is involved in transcendence. This happened along lines made predictable by the Incarnation itself. But now it was made palpable via a heightened awareness of the Communion of Saints. In his saints—so ordinary people and the great doctors could agree—God has come exceptionally close to us.

The case of Martin de Porres illustrates this well. There's plenty of divine power around: well-attested visions, ecstasies, bilocation, infused theological knowledge, miraculous cures, preternatural control over animals. But this divine power was expressed in a reassuringly unthreatening human life: a mulatto boy, illegitimate at a time when it mattered, an endearing child who gave away everything he was given, devoted to a medical apostolate among the poor on the basis of an early apprenticeship to a doctor.

Considering himself unfitted to have the status and rights of a lay-brother, he was for years a kind of auxiliary without any institutional claim on the Dominican Order. After nine years they insisted, and made him indeed spiritual director of the ordained brethren. He called himself 'poor slave', 'mulatto dog'; he was called 'father of charity', 'the father of the poor'.

Now the votive candles blaze out for him in walls of fire, showing that the consciousness of the patristic Church is still alive and well in the faith and devotion of the people.

4 November, St Charles Borromeo

We remember today one of the outstanding figures of the reform of the Church which followed the Council of Trent: St Charles Borromeo. His emergence was an example, I suppose, of the Pauline maxim about how all things work together unto good for those who love God. Charles was catapulted into prominence by the old-boy or rather 'old uncle' network of Renaissance nepotism. His mother's brother—they came from the great Florentine family of the Medici—became pope as Pius IV, and at the age of twenty-two Charles found himself a doctor of divinity, a lay cardinal and acting head of the Roman Curia. For once it paid off. His energy and diplomatic gifts kept the Council of Trent on the road. He took a major part in drafting its excellent Catechism. And he was responsible for much in the subsequent revision of the Liturgy and Church music: he was the patron of Palestrina.

In 1564 when Charles was twenty-six he was ordained to the priesthood and, in quick succession, the episcopate, becoming archbishop of Milan. The following year, on Pius IV's death, he gained permission from the Dominican pope Pius V to do what he really wanted, which was to reside in his diocese. It seems, we might think, a modest ambition for a bishop and yet none had done so at Milan for eighty years. Charles began his reign there by giving away most of his revenue to the poor. He then turned to the spiritual and governmental galvanizing of the Milanese church, devoting himself especially to the Christian education of the young and the formation of future priests. He took seriously Trent's injunction that the chief duty of a bishop is to preach. He visitated every corner of his diocese including physically dangerous bits of the Alps and back in his cathedral city nursed plague victims and fed the starving during the epidemics that hit Lombardy in the 1570s. His reforms met with vigorous opposition from the civil authorities and Religious Orders, and there was an attempt to assassinate him.

Charles Borromeo had an English connexion. He kept always with him a picture of St John Fisher. He died at Milan on the night of the 3rd of November and, entirely appropriately, is buried in its cathedral. At the end of the twentieth century, Blessed John Paul II made clear his view that Charles Borromeo is still the model for what a diocesan bishop should be.

7 November, All Saints of the Order of Preachers

We keep today the great family festival of the Order of Preachers. A family is a wonderful thing, and it can also be a terrible thing, according to the old adage, 'The corruption of the best is the worst'. The thing about families is the way they perpetuate themselves. They can master time by handing down not just memories (how Aunt Hilda fell off the South Pier at Brighton) but also attitudes, practices, ways of doing things. And while this can be wonderful it can also be awful. In dysfunctional families, child-abuse or wife-beating or petty criminality or just plain emotional coldness can be handed on from one generation to another.

A Religious Order could easily be a dysfunctional family where incomers were spoiled by the acquired habits of the existing members. It could easily be that if it weren't for today's feast, which celebrates all the Order's blesseds and saints. The latter stop us getting too obsessed by wiping smear-marks from the refectory table and instead they make us look at the stars.

When we look there, what do we find? At first sight, a bewildering array of different kinds of inspiration, so different as to be incapable of emulation. What is there in common between a University professor with a European reputation like Albert the Great and an obscure recluse who spent her life in a cell attached to a church wall like Hosanna of Kotor? Or between a revivalist preacher like Vincent Ferrer, always on the move, accompanied by his schola for singing the Masses at which he addressed thousands, and a contemplative nun like Catherine de' Ricci lost in mental absorption in the Passion of Christ?

What is in common among our saints and blesseds and, in this sense, what is the unity of this spiritual family?

It turns, I think, on two principles one of which we can conveniently attach to St Dominic and the other to St Thomas. First, thanks to St Dominic, this is an Order where the end or aim is apostolic preaching but where the life is primarily contemplative in kind. All Dominicans are or should be equally at home with the apostolate and with contemplation. For us, preaching is the effect of contemplation and contemplation is never without its overflow in intercessory concern for the Church and the world.

Secondly, thanks to St Thomas, this Order has a view of the supernatural as generous as its view of the natural. Thomas taught us to respect creation in all its forms, and not least the human mind. Chesterton remarked of Thomas that if, like Carmelites, Dominicans took titles of devotion, he would be Thomas *de Creatore*, Thomas 'of the Creator'. Dominicans value natural reason and theological study. But that is not Thomas's ultimate secret any more than it is that of All Saints of the Order of Preachers. This Order has the highest possible estimation of grace, and the way the realm of grace so exceeds the realm of nature that there is no real proportion between them. Nothing in nature prepares us for the discovery of the sheer amplitude of the gift of grace which is, by the Saviour's gift, real participation in the love-exchange of the Holy Trinity.

That is why Dominican saints can spend their lives in rapture before the abundance of salvation as well as write scholarly treatises about it. And when they do write those treatises what they value most about them is not the procedures of natural reason they employ, or even the theological study in the light of faith which they involve. What they most value is any symptom they carry of the infused wisdom, the Wisdom from above, that produces on earth the 'savouring' knowledge which comes from loving contemplation of divine things.

8 November, All Souls of the Order of Preachers

Yesterday we remembered in one celebration all the Dominican saints and blesseds, and asked for their prayers since we need all the help we can get. They amount to a couple of hundred people whose lives proceeded and ended in such fervour of mind and heart for God and the salvation of their neighbour that they were subsequently acclaimed as holy. They were recognized as reproducing in their lives the basic set, if you like, of the personality of our Lord himself, who is the Paradigm of sanctity. As we put it in the Gloria of the Mass: *Tu solus Sanctus*: 'You alone are the Holy One'.

To this extent, despite outward diversity of circumstances and tasks, the saints are all alike. At the opening of *Anna Karenina* Tolstoy remarks, 'All happy families are alike. All unhappy families are different.'

Today, we turn our attention instead to the rest of the Order's dead, a throng whom no man can number, and whose lives proceeded and ended, for the most part, in an ambiguity so many-sided and individual that Tolstoy's maxim applies to them quite well. Largely, this is a matter of varying shades of mediocrity, bearing in mind that the nature of Religious life makes it both easier to rise and easier to fall. Those who found it easier to fall have the advantage that we can enter into solidarity with them since often enough we are like them. To suppose it is easier to understand St Thomas or St Catherine than to understand the anonymous frail ones is an illusion. The saints have so purified their motives and characters that they are detached from us not in reality but in our perceiving. They go forward into the light which absorbs them into its own radiance. We are left with the uninspired, the compromised, the spiritually confused, in a fraternity where things are equal. We pray for them as they, we hope, pray for us: scraps and rags of prayer in each case, yet effective since made in the single Mediator and Atoner for the sins of all the world whose title is 'Holy One', but whose name is Jesus, meaning: 'The Lord saves'.

9 November, The Dedication of the Lateran Basilica

Symbols are very concrete. And so we often contrast them with ideas, which are abstract. But this contrast is a bit over-simplistic. A modern philosopher has said that symbols are what give rise to thought. Certainly the symbols that are the Church's great feasts in the Liturgy give us plenty to think about.

So much so that there generally isn't time on the day to do it properly. And so new commemorations arise to give us the opportunity to mull over things we might have missed on the feast. For example, the feast of Christ the King, soon approaching, enables us to take in better what happened on the great feast of the Ascension. And now today, the Dedication of the Lateran Basilica, serves to underline one important aspect of the feast of the two principal apostles, St Peter and St Paul.

We celebrate today the particular aspect of the apostolic work of Peter and Paul, but especially Peter, which leads us to call the church that witnessed their martyrdom a church that enjoys universal primacy: a church which ranks first in the hierarchy of the churches, the diocesan churches, in a way that ought to affect all Christians, whether it does so or not. At the end of the first century, St Ignatius of Antioch wrote that the church that presides in the country of the Romans 'presides in love' over all the churches. And fifty years later St Irenaeus of Lyons added that this is the church with whose faith 'all other churches must agree'.

What these texts tell us is that the church of the city of Rome is not just one more of the many local churches that makes up the Catholic Church like Milan or Rouen or East Anglia. Instead, it represents the role of Peter in the midst of the apostles, the Peter to whom whatever was given to the apostles was given personally, and in advance.

It is because the Roman church represents the ministry of Peter, confirming his brethren, that its significance extends into all the other local churches of the Catholic world. The Creeds tacitly take this for granted. The Church of Jesus Christ is one, holy, catholic and apostolic, but it is also Petrine and therefore Roman. Without the church that holds the place of Peter there couldn't be a full realization of what our Lord intended for his community.

And so we can call ourselves 'Roman' Catholics even if we've never been further south than Dover. In every Mass we commemorate the pope by name to remind us of that. And similarly, every church building in which we worship bears a relation to the cathedral of St John Lateran, the cathedral of the church of Rome, 'mother and head' of the churches. When you walk into any Catholic church or chapel, you are always immediately related to the basilica that sits atop the Lateran hill.

Yes, today's celebration makes us think about our communion with the holy apostles.

10 November, St Leo

As the days draw in and the chill of a Northern winter begins to creep up on us, the Liturgy for a brief while looks south, to the warmer clime of oleanders and lemon groves and scurrying lizards, beneath the plash of fountains, from which regions our faith came to us, whether directly or indirectly. We look in other words to the only apostolic see in the West, to Rome. Yesterday, the feast of the Dedication of the Lateran Basilica, we were thinking about the mystery of the Church, and the way that mystery finds embodiment in a world-wide institution, an institution that has its own centre of communion in the cathedral church of the see of Peter. Today, the memorial of the greatest of the popes of the patristic age, St Leo, we recall Leo's testimony to the special place in Christendom of the church of Peter notably via his teaching that the preaching of Peter's successor is a sacrament (in the wide sense of that word, an outward and visible sign) of Peter's preaching in the Church.

In a way, however, that is only an aspect or an example albeit an important one of a broader principle which can be formulated by saying that everything that is visible in the work of our Redeemer (including then Christ's appointment of St Peter to a special ministry) has 'passed into the mysteries' — passed over, that is, into the sacramental Liturgy of the church. Just as Jesus Christ is the personal expression of the mystery of God and his actions express the mystery of his person, so the Liturgy of the Church in turn expresses those actions from Annunciation to Pentecost by which our Lord brought the mystery of God to bear salvifically on the world.

The Liturgy is a presence in mystery, in sacred signs, of those perennially valid and fruitful actions by which God willed his own Trinitarian life to be poured out onto the world. So the Redeemer's gift to us of the Church at large, and of the Petrine ministry in particular, must always be seen in the widest context. It is the pope preaching week in, week out, the truths of faith in his episcopal city as he celebrates the liturgical round of the Christian year, rather than his exceptional acts in defining doctrine, that principally show us Peter still continuing his commission among us.

11 November, St Martin of Tours

Martin of Tours was one of the most popular saints of the English Middle Ages. You can see that from the way his cult became intertwined with the rhythms of the economy and the rhythms of nature. Martinmas was a time for hiring people so as to provide employment for the onset of winter; it was also a time for killing and salting cattle, in order to lay down food for winter supplies. In iconography his emblem was a goose, since the migration of flocks of geese from the Arctic North happened around his day, a period often marked (it was said) by a spell of fine weather ('St Martin's summer'). It was a time on the boundary between summer and the solar winter.

These were rather homely ways in which to remember a saint who had done a lot of impressive things. He had pioneered monasticism in the West and used it to transform the moral quality of the episcopate in Gaul. He had stood out against the Roman army over conscientious objection. He had opposed the Roman emperor over the civil punishment of Christian heretics. He had worked well-attested miracles, not least the miracle of charity summed up in the famous story of his giving half his cloak to a beggar. Those who knew the lives of the saints (and mediaeval preaching and sacred art made sure people *did* know them) could, then, hook those major features of Martin's life onto the pegs of custom in farmyard and folklore.

It was in fact the achievement of mediaeval Christianity to incarnate in ordinary ways figures, who in themselves were extraordinary, who went beyond the world of their time or even any time. So grace could seem natural and nature seem gracious, the two enfolded in each other without the one collapsing into the other.

One of our principal tasks today is to re-build a working Christian culture of this kind.

12 November, St Josaphat

Today's saint, Josaphat, was a seventeenth century Orthodox bishop murdered for his attempts to re-unite the Russian church with Rome.

On the borderlands between Russia and Poland, where a Russian-speaking Orthodox peasantry was governed by a Polish-speaking Catholic aristocracy, it was a risky undertaking. No one imposed it on him; it was freely adopted: it was, he held, his mission, and a mission carries duties. It was from a sense of those duties that Josaphat begged his murderers not to touch his serv-ants. So they avoided a general *mêlée*, stunned him with a halberd and shot him instead.

From Josapahat comes that brave 'Greek-Catholic' church of the Ukraine whose archbishop-major, previously based at Lviv, now has his cathedral in Kiev.

In recent years the Papacy has admitted that 'Uniatism', defined as the reconciliation of some part of an Orthodox church with Rome, is not an ideal solution to the problem of disunity. For while in some cases it has created bridges, and proved that one can be in Catholic communion without losing anything or at any rate anything crucial in the Eastern Christian heritage, in others it has bred new suspicion and resentment.

Will the ecumenical movement of modern times succeed better than the Uniatist endeavours of the Crusading period onwards? An observer might not be too optimistic. Perhaps it requires that unflagging prayer with which the petitioner of our Lord's parable wore down the unjust Judge. If so, it lies beyond the calculations of ecumenical strategists.

15 November, St Albert

Albert was a German Dominican of the thirteenth century who in 1931 was named patron of natural science thanks to his treatises on a variety of topics in which he combined acute observation with often correct theorizing.

For instance, Albert noted the effect of latitude on climate; he believed the earth to be not only spherical but inhabited throughout except at the poles (owing to their coldness); he held that the Milky Way was composed of myriads of stars. He realized the influence of light and temperature on the height and spread of trees, and was the first person to describe accurately the behaviour of many European animals, birds and insects. Albert, it pleases me to note, had his own cat, presumably a foundling, since it was called 'Sine Nomine': 'The Nameless One'.

His naturalism, however, was contained within a metaphysical and mystical vision which came to him from orthodox Christianity and the culture it had produced. His spirituality was consistently centred on God. He called it in fact 'the application of all affective and intellectual faculties for the purpose of knowing divine things with sweetness of heart and rapture of mind'. His theology and spirituality were, moreover, deeply embedded in the life and service of the Church, especially when he was made bishop of Regensburg, and sought to restore the primitive ideal of the bishop as shepherd, divesting his office of the temporal and even military duties it had acquired under feudalism.

In 1276 while giving a lecture Albert's memory failed and he suffered almost total amnesia. So in the end the informational knowledge and the conceptual apparatus he had built up over a lifetime fell away, leaving his spirit conformed to the crucified Lord whom he celebrated in his biblical commentaries and sermons. In this way he experienced that 'narrow gate' spoken of in the Gospels. It is a gate through which not only natural but even supernatural endowment must be made small so as to enter.

17 November, St Elizabeth of Hungary

Elizabeth of Hungary has entered the General Calendar of the Roman Church as a representative of all the holy queens of Christendom, especially those who gave themselves to the service of the poor.

Strictly speaking, however, Elizabeth was not a queen though she was a king's daughter. Her husband was the Landgrave of Thuringia and so, while a ruler, he was only a prince. Their marriage appears to have been idyllic. He put no obstacle in the way of her many and increasing charities, or of her life of devotion generally. When she heard the news of his sudden death, from the plague he had contracted in Italy just as he was preparing to leave for the Crusades, she reacted very much like Queen Victoria at the death of Prince Albert: running unstoppably about the corridors not of Windsor but of the Wartburg and shrieking like someone crazed.

In the spring of 1228 Ludwig of Thuringia's body was brought home, and that Good Friday Elizabeth took the habit of the Friars Minor as a Franciscan tertiary. She spent the rest of her life serving the sick and the poor in their homes and in a hospice she had built near Marburg, fishing in nearby streams to raise extra money for their needs, and treated dreadfully (so far as one can tell) by her spiritual director.

She was twenty-four when she died, late on the evening of 17 November 1231. 'It is now the time', she told her attendant, when He rose from the grave and broke the doors of hell, and He will release me'. In 1539, another landgrave, Luther's supporter Philip of Hesse, removed her relics from their much frequented shrine at Marburg to a place that is still unknown.

If this is how the Lord deals with his friends, then, as Teresa of Avila with her usual acerbity told God, it is not surprising there are so few of them. But, I fear, it is part of being a saint to say, Come what must, may his adorable will be done.

20 November, St Edmund

St Edmund's birthplace is unknown but it must have been somewhere where kings of East Anglia ruled, and he would be the last of the East Anglian royal line. It was his misfortune as it was also his glory that his reign coincided with invasion, led by the pagan Ingvar of Denmark. Travelling east from the Midlands in the year 870, the Danes routed Edmund's force and caught up with the fugitive and his retinue at Helledon, an area of woodland near Norwich, where the king had a lodge or hall.

The terms of surrender were commonplace for the time: Edmund could stay on if he handed over half his treasure and ruled as a sub-king under the overlordship of the Danes. A bishop who was his chaplain urged him to accept, but he demurred. Submission would devalue the sacrifice of those already killed and desecrate his own Baptism, Confirmation and kingly anointing. He would only agree if Ingvar accepted Baptism. 'Otherwise', so runs the text of the narrative of his martyrdom, 'I would rather be a standard-bearer in the camp of the Eternal King'.

He was disarmed, bound, tied to a tree and beaten so badly that, we are told, it seemed an animal had mauled him. His calling on Christ enraged the Danes who shot at him till his body bristled with arrows, the arrows he would later be portrayed with in the sacred images. Then he was wrenched from the tree and his head struck off. The pagans left the body in the wood but took the head, which Edmund's attendants supposed they would throw away to be eaten by birds or animals. It was found later that day unharmed between the paws of a wolf.

Whatever one makes of that as a sign of sanctity it is historical fact that paganism failed to recover ground in East Anglia in the way it did in other areas of the Danish settlement. When in 877 Alfred the Great inflicted their first defeat on the pagan incomers, the Danish chieftain in East Anglia accepted the Baptism his predecessor had refused. In 886 there was minted the first of a series of coins bearing Edmund's name for this area of mixed

English and Danish population. Fifty years later, Edmund's relics were transferred to a great timber church at Beodricsworth in Suffolk, subsequently re-named Bury St Edmunds.

Where is he now? After the death of Richard I Plantagenet the dauphin of France was a principal contender for the throne of England. His main English ally, the earl of Winchester, seized the relics of St Edmund in his flight to France in 1216. They were taken on the anti-Albigensian Crusade and found a home in the city of Toulouse. In 1901 Cardinal Vaughan asked the pope to order that the relics should come to Westminster, to be enshrined in the high altar of the new cathedral. They were to be a rival presence to St Edward down the road at the abbey. Reluctantly, the archbishop of Toulouse allowed the body to come to England, but no sooner had it arrived than *The Times* stirred up a controversy about the authenticity of the remains. Despite the positive findings of a French commission of enquiry in 1902, it was thought more politic to lock them away in the vaults of Arundel Castle, home of the 'premier Catholic layman', the Duke of Norfolk, where they remain till this day.

No matter. We have the example of his courage, his determination not to let the faith be subordinated to any other religion, ideology, or system of rule. He is *the* holy intercessor of East Anglia. May his prayers avail us now.

21 November, The Presentation of the Blessed Virgin Mary

The evangelists don't have much information to offer about the early life of our Lady, but the modern scholars (at least of the sort I read) can help. She was a Nazarene, which is now understood to mean an inhabitant of the 'village of the branch', *natzor*, a reference to the shoot that would spring from the Rod of Jesse: in other words, to the messianic hope of the Jewish people. Nazareth, it seems, had been founded only a century or so before Mary's birth by families of Jews returning to the Holy Land from the Diaspora, probably from Babylon, where they had retained the memory of their Davidide origin: their descent from king David.

In the Magnificat, Mary's self-identification with the poor and dispossessed and with the spirituality of humble dependence on God for everything (that runs through all the sayings ascribed to her), becomes more explicable against this background of a largely forgotten and perhaps somewhat despised or even slightly absurd once royal extended family. 'Can anything good come out of Nazareth?'

Her vow of sexual continence, implied in her response at the Annunciation ('How can this be since I know not man [i. e. I am not to know man]?') suggests that her kinsfolk had gravitated towards the Essene movement, for the Essenes were the only Jews who understood and practised serious asceticism, including, in many cases, dedicated virginity. The same influence is seen in the career of her cousin, John the Baptist, and indeed, in certain respects, in what we learn of Mary's Son.

But that, if we are right, did not mean that Mary went all the way with the Essenes: for instance—and this is the point at issue in today's memorial—in their complete repudiation of the Jerusalem Temple and its worship. In the canonical Gospels, she goes there herself for purification, presenting her Son as the first-born, and Jesus would continue to frequent the Temple he had cleansed. Today's commemoration is based on a non-canonical writing preserved by the early Church. Along with some very implausible claims, it may well enshrine a genuine memory, treasured by Jewish-Christians of the first generation. That Mary's parents should have brought her to Zion, to the great Temple built originally by David's son, and the haunt, still, of those who expected the Messiah, people like Anna and Simeon, is credible enough.

The deeper meaning of today's feast, however, is that the woman who is to be the true Temple of the divine Glory, the future mother of the Messiah, comes to that place where the Glory dwelt provisionally in a building of wood and stone. Mary's Child is to be not merely the tabernacle of the Glory, but the very Glory itself: God from God, Light from Light, as we say in the Creed. And that cannot but have implications for how we think of Mary, the Mother of the Lord.

22 November, St Cecilia

St Cecilia is most famous as the patron of musicians. This is a very
late development in her cultus: it doesn't seem to have been known
before the sixteenth century. She was one of those woman martyrs
in the Roman empire who were punished for refusing to enter
marriage with high-ranking pagans: our own Geoffrey Chaucer
tells the story and an antiphon in the fifth century Acts of her life
gave people a thousand years later the idea of a musical connexion.
'As the organs [at her wedding feast] were playing, Cecilia sang
in her heart to the Lord.'

It proved a very successful idea. In the 1680s and '90s both John
Dryden and Alexander Pope wrote poems to be set to music for St
Cecilia's day, knowing perhaps that in 1584 she had become the
patroness of the newly established Academy of Sacred Music in
Rome: the *Accademia di Santa Cecilia*, now the seat of one of the
main Italian orchestras.

In modern Italy, Church music is rarely anything to write home
about, but in England sacred music of a serious and worthy kind
is one of the main links between Church and culture and for many
people, if only through CDs, keeps the sense of transcendence alive
where otherwise it might have disappeared. In her novel *The Choir*
the popular contemporary novelist Joanna Trollope muses, 'St Paul
had known about music and God. Join together, he had told the
early Christians, join together singing and making melody to the
Lord. Nothing was more powerful than music, nothing more
uniting [she goes on, putting words into the mouth of the head-
master of a choir school threatened with closure], nothing lifted
man in worship as music could, the voice of the trumpet calling
out, "Come up hither, Come up to me"'.

As those last phrases suggest, music is an important image of
final salvation, when everything in us that is adamant against God
will be softened and liquefied and through grace turn into sheer
praise. John Donne, the English metaphysical poet, hoped for this
on his death-bed: 'I am coming to that holy room/ where, with thy
Quire of Saints for evermore/ I shall be made thy Music'. Beautiful,
but we offer the Mass and struggle to live the Christian life because
of the warning, delicately expressed yet unmistakable, by which

Donne follows up these words: 'As I come/ I tune the instrument here at the door,/ And what I must do then, think here before'.

24 November, The Korean Martyrs

Until 1910 all of Korea was as cut off from the rest of the world as Burma tried to be yesterday. From the end of the sixteenth century no foreigner was permitted to live there and only once a year could any Koreans go abroad: to Beijing, to pay a ceremonial tax to the Chinese emperor. No wonder the country was known as the 'Hermit Kingdom'.

How, then, did Catholicism arise there? In an historically unique way. The first Korean Catholics were entirely self-taught in their religion, which they learned in books brought back from Beijing where a member of the annual delegation had been baptized by a French Jesuit. That was in 1783. Less than twenty years later, there was already a Korean church of two thousand souls, three hundred of whom were put to death in 1801.

Throughout the nineteenth century the Korean monarchy persecuted the Church with sporadic severity. The one hundred and five martyrs of Korea we celebrate today come from the persecutions of 1839, 1846 and 1866-to-1869, in the latter of which about ten thousand Catholics were executed. Three of the one hundred and five holy martyrs were French: one bishop and two priests who had entered the country clandestinely and adopted Korean names and dress. The rest were Koreans; with one exception, all were laymen and laywomen.

The Church in South Korea today is perhaps the fastest growing in the Catholic world. Though the North remains behind a bamboo curtain, it is likely that eventually we shall see there the words of Tertullian vindicated, 'The blood of martyrs is the seed of the Church'. Or in the words of Walter Shewring's fine twentieth century hymn:

> From thee the martyrs, we from those,
> Each in thy grace's measure spring.
> Their strength upon our weakness flows
> And guides us to the goal we sing.

25 November, St Catherine of Alexandria

Today is one of those celebrations where we have to rely on the Church's memory and intuition rather than historical sources. Tradition reports that Catherine of Alexandria was a high-ranking Christian who lived in a time of persecution under the emperor Maxentius. Her faith, along with a promise of consecrated virginity, stood in the way of an imperial marriage, so fifty philosophers were convoked to convince her of its falsity. She refuted their arguments and thus precipitated her own execution. As originally planned, this was to be by breaking on a wheel. But the apparatus collapsed, injuring bystanders, and she was beheaded instead.

Pope Paul VI removed St Catherine from the General Calendar of the Latin church but Pope John Paul II restored her, undoubtedly because she was the patron of philosophers. That was also, incidentally, why mediaeval Dominicans revered her.

Execution is an abrupt way of breaking off an argument and philosophy is not for the impatient. Philosophy is the attempt to take into consideration the totality of what we meet with in reality. To be treated philosophically, a topic, however concrete or limited, must be viewed against the backdrop of the whole of reality and it has to be considered under every possible aspect. That's why philosophy is wider and more foundational than the sciences and arts. The key to the philosophical mentality is that not one single aspect of reality be suppressed or forgotten.

That is also why philosophizing is important to the Church. Philosophy prevents theology and preaching from becoming narrow, from just homing in time and again on the same few biblical themes, or themes of Christian living, without taking thought for all the perspectives that open up, not least for those themes, by taking a wider view.

But can someone become a saint by being a philosopher? Well, why shouldn't a philosopher ask, Has a divine act of communication been made to human beings, perhaps at their origin, or perhaps in history? If so, has it been kept historically present through the generations? Is it found in the act of faith by which the human person accepts divine speech as a word of truth? If so, then this too belongs with the consideration of the totality of all we meet with in reality. If so, once again, someone faithful to it until death is a philosopher-martyr, a philosopher-saint. This is what we claim, in point of fact, for today's saint.

30 November, St Andrew

Andrew, brother of Peter, came from Bethsaida which is now about half a mile to the north of the Sea of Galilee. In those days, however, it was at the spot where the waters of the Jordan joined the Lake, and so a great place to fish. In fact its name, Bethsaida, could be translated literally as 'Fishingborough'.

When with the Gospels we remember that Andrew was a fisherman by trade, we must be careful not to overdo the 'simple unlettered man' business. There is a lot to know about fishing in the Sea of Galilee: a great variety of species, and of possible interactions of current and climate. Moreover, we need to bear in mind that first century Palestine was not a meritocracy, where everyone quasi-automatically finds their own level. The fact that Andrew, as we hear in St John's Gospel, was instrumental in introducing to the Saviour a party of Greeks—sophisticated internationalized outsiders, whether Jewish or pagan—suggests they had looked Andrew over and found him a sympathetic and intelligent intermediary: no mere country bumpkin.

All the main figures of the Gospels possess certain structural relations to our Lord, relationships which act as vehicles of revelation and as such are woven into the later fabric of the Church. Just as Jesus would not be the saving revelation of the Father in the way he is without a relation to Mary, to the Baptist, the beloved disciple, and so forth, so he would not be what he is without his relation to the apostles, his intimate circle. And although Andrew has been taken as their patron by a variety of countries from Russia to Scotland, the Church came to remember him primarily as the apostle of Byzantium, the apostle of the Greeks. That is why today, 30 November, the pope will have sent an envoy to Constantinople with greetings, just as on 29 June, the feast of the apostles Peter and Paul the Ecumenical Patriarch sends an envoy to Rome.

The historical value of the first accounts of the link between St Andrew and missionary work in the area of the original Byzantium is somewhat in question. But what is not questionable is the insight of faith that by his intercession Andrew continues to bring 'Greeks' to Jesus, as once he did at Capernaum: that, in other words, he stands for the capacity of the Church to initiate into the mystery of Jesus the sophistication, the expertise, the know-how, of the world, and to let the world find there the beauty, truth and goodness for which it was made.

DECEMBER

3 December, St Francis Xavier

Francis Xavier is the patron of Catholic missions. Missionising is one of the things we have to do between the lightning flash and the thunderclap, between the Incarnation and the Parousia. Not that we have to do it in his amazing way, moving in the space of a decade from life as son of the castle-dwelling classes in the area roughly of the Pyrenees to living in a hut, off rice and water, sleeping on the ground among low-caste peoples in Sri Lanka, south India, the Moluccas and Malaya. In Japan he changed his strategy. He wore fine robes and presented costly ingenious gifts—clocks and musical boxes—to the Mikado. Everywhere his zeal and persistence (he had no natural flair for languages and was a bad sailor) and his striking God-centredness were met with a response which critical historians have been unable to deconstruct.

Yet he considered his life to have been a failure: he never got to the country he believed himself called to evangelise, China, dying on an island off the Chinese coast, looking across to the forbidden territory. It is all evidenced in the many volumes of his correspondence. Yet I do not believe Hollywood could have invented a more dramatic ending.

4 December, St John Damascene

St John of Damascus is a good saint and doctor to celebrate as Christmas draws near. His name will always be bound up with the defence of the icons, the holy images, against those who wanted to eliminate sacred art root and branch as no better than idolatry. And the most important plank in Damascene's defence of the icons was that since the Incarnation, since the first Christmas, everything is different.

The Jews had been forbidden by the Second Commandment from making images of God on the basis of anything creaturely. But now with the Incarnation God had made himself manifest, made himself visible, made himself visually accessible to us, by himself assuming a creature's life. God has taken something creaturely, an instance of our humanity, the manhood of Jesus Christ, and he has united it to himself as the expression of his own divine being. So through something creaturely, and even something material indeed, the human body, God has (if you like) shown his hand.

And not only his hand, but more than that, his Face: the Face that, in the Psalms of Ascent people said they longed and longed to see as they went up to worship at the Temple. Yes, God has laid bare his personal mystery as he worked out our salvation in all the scenes where the Word incarnate put in an appearance from the crib of Bethlehem to Golgotha and the encounters with the Risen One. 'I do not worship matter', wrote St John, 'but I venerate him who for my sake became material and through matter worked out my salvation.'

So in the Church holy images are not just the ecclesiastical equivalent of wallpaper. They are a statement of dogma, a confession of our faith in the invisible God who entered visibility for our sake. The icons portray above all the One who will be born at Christmas though they also show the relations the incarnate Son enjoys with our Lady and all the saints in the outworking of salvation in history, in the world.

6 December, St Nicholas

There are a variety of weird and wonderful—but mostly wonderful—legends about St Nicholas of Myra, a fourth century bishop in what is now Turkey and one of the most popular saints in the Eastern, and especially the Byzantine-rite, Church (and therefore among the Eastern Orthodox and not just Catholics).

Threes play a large part in the *legendarium*: three sailors rescued from a storm, three men saved from unjust execution, three murdered children miraculously raised to life. But considered as a saint for the approach of Christmastide the most important of these traditions is surely Nicholas' provision of dowries for three poor girls enabling them to marry: in each case a bag of gold lobbed anonymously through their father's window. In the south and east of Europe that was taken as just another example of the resourcefulness and ingenuity of the charity of St Nicholas. But in the north—in Germany, Switzerland, and the Netherlands—the three bags were singled out for special emphasis and, though sometimes confused, rather gruesomely, with the missing heads of the three murdered children, became the basis of a new popular image for this saint: Nicholas as the holy bishop who delights to give secret gifts to children.

When that folk legend crossed the Atlantic with Teutonic immigrants in the course of the nineteenth century it became Americanised in the figure of Santa Claus, and in due time (I regret to say) 'Disneyfied': turned into a cartoon character in a baggy red suit and improbable beard with a fleet of airborne reindeers and a penchant for slipping down chimneystacks, when (that is) he was not putting up his feet somewhere in Lapland for the rest of the year outside of Christmas. This was the figure that in the twentieth century was exported back to Europe to became the centre-piece of Santa's Grotto at Harrod's and doubtless the equivalent superstores in Hamburg, Zurich or Amsterdam. Thus far has fallen our father among the saints the God-loving hierarch and thaumaturge Nicholas.

Yet if we can manage to lift ourselves for a moment from out of this bubble bath of sentimentality we should be able to discern an important theological message. In focusing on gift, and especially on secret gift, the Christian imagination did not, to that extent, go astray. Creation, life, *is* a gift, and it is even a secret gift as the existence of atheists proves. The Incarnation resembles creation in that respect (no one is compelled by the evidence for it), bearing in that way the hallmark of the authentically divine.

> He came all so still
> where his Mother was
> as dew in April
> that falleth on the grass.

May Santa Claus, Sankt Niklaus, forgive us what we have done to him and bring us this Christmas an understanding of these mysteries.

7 December, St Ambrose

St Ambrose became bishop of Milan in a rather unusual manner. In the fourth century the city was divided between Arians who denied the divinity of Christ and Catholics who affirmed it. Ambrose had been trained as a lawyer and administrator, and had made a fairly meteoric rise to governorship of an Italian Province when he appeared, still a catechumen, in the main basilica of Milan at the time when a new bishop had to be chosen. In the face of the threat from Arianism it had to be someone good. His election became a famous story. A little boy started calling out *Ambrosius episcopus*, 'Ambrose for bishop', and the cry was taken up by the crowd. Ambrose was brought to the font for a slightly premature Baptism, and ordained bishop a few days later. This is sometimes put forward nowadays as a model for people-power in action in the Church, through we should note how Ambrose took steps to ensure it didn't recur at Milan by nominating his own successor on his death-bed.

He proved a great pastor of the Milanese church which was a prominent one since in this period Milan was the usual place of residence of the Western Roman emperors. Ambrose was firm in his defence of Catholicism against the Arians, vigilant against any possible return of paganism to official status, a fearless critic of a Catholic emperor for his disgraceful massacre of citizens at Thessalonica (Ambrose would not let Theodosius come to Communion until he had done public penance), a tireless preacher and celebrant of the mysteries, and yet he was readily accessible to people of all stations in life.

When we remember him as a doctor of the Church, however, something rather different comes to mind. St Ambrose is an example of 'light from the East': not because he was an Oriental dropped down in the Latin Church for, on the contrary, born at Trier (in what is now Germany), he was an Occidental to his fingertips. But nevertheless he realised the huge riches that lay waiting in the works of such Greek Fathers as St Basil and St Gregory Nazianzen, and the other ecclesiastical writers of the Eastern church, like Origen. Through Ambrose, something of their biblical knowledge, their rigorous doctrinal thinking, and their profound mystical theology entered the West. He evidently believed that the Catholic Church should breathe with her two lungs, Eastern as well as Western. Nothing that has happened

subsequently in the story of the Church, her theology, her spirituality, her Liturgy, suggests that he made a mistake.

8 December, Solemnity of the Immaculate Conception

For a long time before the Church went ahead and defined the
doctrine of the Immaculate Conception, in the mid-nineteenth
century, the Dominicans had a difficulty with it. Except, that is, in
Spain where *la Immacolada* was the national patron. (We are all
influenced by our environments!) Not that, like some modern
Liberal Protestants, the Dominicans thought our Lady was just an
ordinary Palestinian-Jewish lass. They themselves taught a high
doctrine of the divine Motherhood and the personal holiness for
Mary which that Motherhood necessarily involved. They never
associated serious personal sins when we freely choose what is
morally evil with the Ark where Emmanuel, 'God with us', was
coming to dwell.

But, on the other hand, following St Thomas (as it is usually
wise to do), they didn't quite see how Mary could be free from *all*
the consequences of the Fall and thus be all-holy from the first
moment of her existence without compromising the very important
claim that Jesus Christ saves universally, saves all men, women,
and children. For this claim implies that all men, women and
children *need* salvation.

It was the Franciscans who set the Dominicans right on this. On
the two occasions in my life when I've taught alongside Franciscans—in Ethiopia, and then in Oxford—I tried to look into the
writings of their great Scholastic, Blessed John Duns Scotus. I gave
up Scotus was far too difficult. But Blessed John is easy to
understand on this subject at least, and he pointed the way forward
for the Church out of an impasse.

He argues as follows. If the Saviour, the God-man Jesus Christ,
really can redeem us absolutely—if he can redeem us utterly,
perfectly—then there must be at any rate one human being who
is utterly, perfectly, redeemed. There must be at least one human
being who can, as it were, demonstrate that being transformed
totally by the grace of Christ is a real possibility for the rest of us.
And that one perfectly redeemed human being will need to be

liberated from all that makes for sin from the word 'Go!'. He or she will need to exemplify the way God in Jesus Christ can redeem us completely, right down to the very roots of our being.

And there's no difficulty about identifying who that human being might be, who it is that corresponds to that job description. This is exactly what the instinct of faith has always wanted to say about blessed Mary: heaping up praises of her faith, holiness, purity, in an effort to bring this same intuition to expression (if only the theologians would allow it).

So today's celebration is a meaningful one for each of us, and for this reason. If God can so redeem, if Jesus Christ can redeem utterly, perfectly, as he did Mary, then he can change us too. Some sacred images of the Immaculate Conception may be weak and watery, but in itself this Solemnity confronts us with a full-blooded realism about salvation in a way no other feast can. That is why we celebrate today not only our Lady but also, in her and with her, the whole Church's hope of becoming holy and immaculate, having (in the words of St Paul's Letter to the Ephesians) 'no spot or wrinkle or any such thing'.

10 December, Blessed Brian Lacey and the Martyrs of East Anglia

We keep today the memorial of a number of East Anglian laypeople and priests, headed by Blessed Brian Lacey, a Norfolk squire, who were executed for the Catholic faith under the relevant statutes in the reigns of the last Tudor and the first Stuart monarchs.

We know so well the points of doctrine for which they died that we may tire of hearing of them. Perhaps this is why not a great deal is made of the English martyrs in the contemporary Church. So what did they die for?

They died for the Mass: the Holy Eucharist makes present the Sacrifice of Christ with all its effects, for the living and the dead, and so can be pleaded for the salvation of all.

They died for the priesthood: only a validly ordained priest offers sacramentally the redeeming Sacrifice of Christ.

They died for the authority of the Church: in the apostolic succession is found an unbroken line of sacramental commission-

ing from Christ through the apostles to the bishops of today, and
an uninterrupted continuity in Christian doctrine from Christ to
those today who teach in union with the College of bishops and
its head, the successor of Peter.

When we celebrate these martyrs in Advent, we implicitly
consider the relevance of these themes to the Advent hope. How
could we make expectation of the Parousia a major theme in our
lives unless we had confidence in the truth brought into this world
by the Incarnation and the continued accessibility of that truth to
us? How could we sustain that expectation without the continued
strength and illumination provided by the mysticism of the Mass?
It is the Mass above all that maintains our devotion to him until
he comes again.

13 December, St Lucy

St Lucy is one of the more obscure martyrs still left in the General
Calendar of the Church but there she stands, interrupting even the
celebration of Advent as an obligatory memorial and this is
undoubtedly owing to her importance for the early Church. She
is, after all, one of the saints named daily in the Roman Canon.

What is known with security is that she was Sicilian, and died
at Syracuse in a persecution at the end of the third century. Her
cultus spread to Rome and Byzantium, as also to England where
the Anglo-Saxon church writer Aldhelm of Sherborne composed
prose and poetry in her honour.

Before the introduction of the Gregorian calendar so throughout
the Western Middle Ages, then St Lucy's day was also, in the terms
of the year of nature, Midwinter Day. 'Lucy's Night' was the
longest night of the year, her day was the shortest day of the year.
But for that very reason her day was also the turn of the year, the
beginning of the end of winter-time. And there is an appropriate
symbolism here. St Lucy's name means 'light' and as the natural
daylight begins to wax again, the Advent season thanks to her
celebration points us to the dawning of supernatural light. In
Christmastide, the true Light will be shining above all on the
Epiphany, the feast of light par excellence when we shall acclaim
the Christ-child in his manifestation to the pagans as Light from

Light, the everlasting radiance of God made bearable to us in the humanity of Jesus and reflected in his saints.

14 December, St John of the Cross

John of the Cross has been admired for combining the gifts of a mystic with those of a poet. This wouldn't be so surprising except for the fact that his ascetic doctrine is so systematic and severe, so very harsh. John recommended that we should detach ourselves as fully as possible from every created good. That is what he calls the 'active night' of the senses and the soul. He thought that really necessary if divine grace is to do its work in us, its work in the corresponding 'passive night' where the Light of God, so overwhelming that we experience it as darkness, enters people and makes them contemplatives.

So the paradox of St John of the Cross is how a teacher with this particular doctrine could also be a lyric poet, expounding in a rapturous way the splendours of all creation.

The key is that what is freely given up is returned to us in a new way. Freed from the world by detachment and purification, the soul is made free for the world which it starts to celebrate, accordingly, in a non-possessive way.

John sees our environment, God's presence to us through nature, as the first approach of the divine Bridegroom. But the final meaning of that takes us beyond nature: it is God's approach to us by grace.

A mystic for Advent, then, as we wait for the Angels to break through the night with the glory of their voices.

26 December, St Stephen

No one seems to know why the feast of Stephen was placed on the 26th of December. It was a very audacious decision. Straight after the Christmas rejoicing we celebrate the proto-martyr, the first Christian martyr. But then we remember that one of the gifts given the Child in the manger was for the anointing of a corpse: 'myrrh his sepulchre foretells'. Our Lord was born to die in a stronger sense than the rest of us. By his death he was, among other things, to show what should be our attitude to life and to death. To life,

Father, forgive them: in other words, compassion; to death, 'Into your hands I commend my spirit': in other words, trust.

Just these qualities were displayed by St Stephen in his martyrdom. And so he points to the meaning of the Babe in the manger just as much as do any of the figures around the Crib.

27 December, St John the Evangelist

On Christmas Day we remind ourselves how at the first Christmas the Word 'became flesh and dwelt among us', the Word who was in the beginning with God in such a way that what God was the Word was. Today we celebrate the person who composed this statement, the evangelist St John.

This is not just association of ideas. When the eternal Word of God took a human nature in which to express himself, he accepted all the conditions of being finite, and one of these is that we are dependent for the image we leave behind of ourselves on the sensitivity and perceptiveness of other people. The Word incarnate lived in a comparatively simple culture, politically marginal and by our standards educationally under-developed. For the most part, he lived among obscure individuals, and not many of them at that.

It took a very special person to discern his glory, 'the glory of the Only Begotten Son of the Father, full of grace and truth'. It took a very special evangelist to discern that glory hidden as it was beneath the lowly façade of its contrary. Humanly speaking, without St John whom the Greeks call 'The Theologian' would the Church have grasped the full significance of the birth of Christ? There could be few better reasons for celebrating any saint now than that.

28 December, The Holy Innocents

We keep today one of the strangest feasts in the Church calendar: 'Childermas', the feast of the Holy Innocents. Though they were not Christians, nor even old enough to be conscious of being Jews, these infants were declared blessed by the Church and poets, preachers and artists have celebrated their memory accordingly.

Subjectively speaking, they did not die for Christ. Objectively speaking, with all the objectivity of the executioner's machete, they did die for him. In fact the Holy Innocents died not only for him but in place of him. They were put to death because of the anxiety his coming aroused in the guilty, and by their deaths he was able to escape and go free.

In a strange way, therefore, the death of the Innocents foreshadowed in its structure the death of Christ himself which was also a vicarious and a substitutionary death. As the New Testament insists in two little Greek words, he died *huper*, for, us, vicariously, and also *anti*, instead of, us, substitutionally. The Innocents herald that process of salvation, from the Incarnation through Calvary to the Resurrection, whereby God in Christ re-established the order of human affairs on himself as centre, creating a new inter-dependence between us at the deepest level possible, both in our sufferings and in our glorification.

So the Holy Innocents are not a strange fluke in the history of sanctity. On the contrary, it is on that interdependence of all our strivings in God that the whole idea and reality of the 'Communion of Saints' actually rests.

And that is why today our minds can travel to those other 'innocents', the modern victims of abortion who died by transgression of the law written on the human conscience, 'You shall not take innocent life'. And it is how we can ask God to treat them as companion martyrs of the Holy Innocents and raise them up to have a share in the vision of himself.

29 December, St Thomas of Canterbury

By the 29th of December it's clear that the Church doesn't try to keep the Octave of Christmas free from the celebration of the saints in the way she keeps the Octave of Easter uncluttered and focussed on the Resurrection of the Crucified. And the reason is: these Christmastide saints' days, which are chiefly the feasts of martyrs, are clues to why the eternal Word became incarnate. More especially, they keep alive the connexion between the Incarnation and the Cross. Even now, in the depths of winter, we look ahead to the destiny of the messianic Child at Easter.

Yesterday we celebrated the deaths of infant martyrs, those who could not speak yet witnessed silently to the Lord who became for us a tiny babe. Today we remember a martyr, Thomas of Canterbury, who by contrast was highly articulate and vocal, and witnessed in argument and debate to the same Lord in another of his states and conditions.

If we ask for what Thomas à Becket died, the immediate answer is he died for the right of the English church to appeal beyond the king, beyond the State, to Rome. But the community of faith, by declaring Becket a martyr, saw more in this than meets the eye. Jesus Christ in his public ministry but above all in his Passion kept himself sovereignly free from the princes and powers of this world. While in no way denying legitimate authority he had let nothing come between him and the Father's purpose. The Church he founded would share this transcendent freedom vis-à-vis the rulers of the world.

The earliest treatise on martyrdom we have is the Apocalypse of St John, and there precisely we see the martyrs defined over against the competing omni-competence of the State: this was how they came to wash their robes in the blood of the Lamb: to take on, we can say, the 'colour' of Christ

And so Becket's death was not only the murder of a stubborn and ambitious cleric. Nor was it simply a death for the primacy of the see of Peter and the close communion between the *Ecclesia anglicana* and Rome which that primacy implies. More than this, it was an act of testimony in Thomas's own dying words, 'for the name of Jesus and for the Church': a confirmation of the mission of Christ in its sovereign independence of the world and the share of the Church, as the messianic community, in that same mission. Chaucer's pilgrims were not deceived as they journeyed to his shrine in Canterbury, 'the holy blissful martyr for to seek'.

CELEBRATIONS IN ORDINARY TIME

Sunday after Pentecost, Solemnity of the Holy and Undivided Trinity (1)

The climax of the Church's year was Pentecost: the descent of the Holy Spirit to found a society of love which will throw open this world to the communion of heaven. That is a pretty hard act to follow even for God. How could we ask for more? In point of fact the feast of the Holy Trinity doesn't try to give us more. Instead, it invites us to sit back and reflect on the presuppositions of what it was that happened to Jesus Christ and through our believing in him by the Holy Spirit, happened to ourselves. This Solemnity invites us to think what sort of reality we must be involved with, if the events that launched the Church into history really occurred.

The feast of the Trinity is not, then, a converting, transforming feast like Easter. Neither is it an ecstatic, enthusiastic feast like Pentecost. Instead, it is a contemplative feast, a feast for reflection, a feast that encourages us to be theologians if only for one day in the year. For this reason Trinity Sunday is a highly unusual kind of feast. Normally, one doesn't throw a party in order to celebrate a presupposition. Yet this is what we are doing today.

Unlike Christmas or the Epiphany, Easter and Pentecost, this Solemnity of the Holy and Undivided Trinity was unknown to the early Church. It was introduced in 1323 by Pope John XXII, an Avignon pope who dabbled in theology and whose thrills and spills with emperors and friars figure in Umberto Eco's best-seller *The Name of the Rose*. The feast of the Trinity stands at the end of a lengthy process of Christian reflection which took centuries to achieve. The Church needed time to work out the implications and the preconditions of the great events that brought her into being, just as we ourselves need time to see the depths and ramifications of the personal events that have shaped our own lives.

Humanly speaking, the first disciples would have been over-whelmed if they had been required to take in the total meaning of the Incarnation and the Redemption in one breath. Intellectually, imaginatively, ethically, they would have had to become super-

men. And because God respects our humanity the apostles were
not expected to grasp immediately all the presuppositions and
further implications of the act of salvation. As our Lord says to
them in one of the Gospels set for today in the Lectionary of Paul
VI: 'I still have many things to say to you, but you cannot bear
them now'.

If we ask what these 'many things' might be, the answer is that
centrally they have to do with what Jesus knew himself to have
been given by my Father. 'All that the Spirit of truth tells you will
be taken from what is mine. Everything the Father has is mine.'
And this is where reflection on God the Holy Trinity might most
usefully begin: Jesus' own relationship with God. The centre of his
relation with God was his awareness of the One whom he called
Abba, a word best translated 'dear Father'. This is the name for God
which originally must have begun the Lord's Prayer, the 'Our
Father', and it was given to the disciples in answer to the request,
'Teach us to pray'.

Though his disciples were believing Jews, they recognized that
in comparison with their Master they could hardly be said to pray
at all. They picked up his knowledge that he stood in a unique
relation of sonship to the *Abba*. His message was the merciful love
of his Father and its nevertheless considerable demands: something
he referred to as 'the Kingdom' of God. And through his ministry
he made this Kingdom, mysteriously bound up as it was with his
own person, accessible to others. As the beloved Son he enjoyed a
unique right of access to the Kingdom but he in turn mediated such
access to his friends as his supreme gift to them, and did so in
power and glory when the Crucified was risen from the dead. As
he put it, 'No one knows the Father but the Son and anyone to
whom the Son chooses to reveal him'.

Now One who brings us God must himself be divine. This is
the foundation of the Church's faith in the Godhead of the Son.
The God beyond us, the Father, is made accessible by Emmanuel,
God-with-us, the Son.

What, then, of the Holy Spirit? Jesus had also been aware of a
unique endowment of the Spirit of God. For Jews, the Spirit
represented the highest possible union between God and man. It
was the breath of the Lord, rousing people to spiritual life. The Son

knew the Spirit to be a Power working in and through him. In his capacity to draw others into his own relation with the Father, to give them a share in the joy of the Kingdom, he could see the singular way in which he possessed the Spirit and the Spirit possessed him. The Spirit was the secret Power behind the *Abba* prayer which united him to the Father. It was also the Power which or, better, who enabled him to draw to the Father those he taught to say the *Abba* prayer.

Now One who brings us to God must himself be divine. And this is the foundation of the Church's faith in the Godhead of the Holy Spirit. God the Spirit draws us to the Son and as he does so makes us like our Lord in his relation with the Father.

So, the 'presupposition' we celebrate today is the relationship going on forever in God, the relationship in which God has offered us a share by taking us into the inner dialogue of Son and Father through the Holy Spirit. It is the ceaseless exchange of giving, receiving, and giving again, that takes place between Father, Son and Spirit from all eternity.

And since for Scripture we are made to be in the image of God and through the saving work of Christ can be effectively re-made in that same image, this tells us of our own destiny. In our better moments we all have intimations of how interchange is the key to our existence. To be receptive we must be outgoing. To accept others, something of ours must be surrendered. Such surrender is not a lessening of our being but its transformation. In a mysterious way, self-transcendence is self-affirmation. It is not the egoists who grow but the sacrificers, not those who take in order to keep but those who receive in order to give again. Just look at the lives of the saints. The Holy Trinity is the ultimate explanation of this condition, for we were made to be its icons.

Sunday after Pentecost, Solemnity of the Holy and Undivided Trinity (2)

The feast of the Holy Trinity is not perhaps the most popular celebration in the Church's year. The Unity in Trinity and Trinity in Unity seems to some to be a mathematical game which diverted mediaeval theologians and doubtless paid their equivalent of milkmen's bills, but has nothing to do with what is called 'real life'. The problem intensifies when we remember that mistakes in Trinitarian doctrine have been regarded by the Church as sufficient to exclude whole groups of people from her communion. The Arians who denied the eternal generation of the Son; the Pneuma- tochians who refused to accept the eternal procession of the Holy Spirit; the Sabellians who regarded both Son and Spirit as mere modes of the Father's being: all of these no doubt sincere and well-meaning people were dropped unceremoniously from the Church's caravan as it moved through history. Even today, a dispute over whether the Spirit proceeds from the Father alone or from the Father and the Son together divides the Catholic and Orthodox Churches. But, the protest runs, if these arcane matters can be made a sufficient reason for keeping human beings apart from each other, do we not need either our heads or our hearts examining or probably both?

Up to a point, such comments are intelligible, but those who make them often have a very weak sense of the importance both spiritually and morally of the Church's doctrine of God. Some people admit to finding the story of Jesus of Nazareth powerful, fascinating, even, but fail to realize that the doctrine of the Trinity is the same story when told in the most profound way possible, at its deepest level of significance.

We get a clue to this in the passage from St John's Gospel which constitutes one of the readings set for this festival in the three-year cycle of texts in the Lectionary of Pope Paul VI. There the doctrine of the Trinity is situated in St John's account of how in his love for the world God sent his only Son so that all might have life through him: a sending which reached its climax on the Cross, thus producing a 'life' flowing from the Resurrection.

On the Cross we see the Holy Trinity for what it is. In the first place, the Son's self-giving there, which summed up his entire previous existence, took place through obedient love of the Father who in his own goodness and mercy had sent the Son. How acceptable that offering of love for the world's salvation was became apparent at the first Easter, in the Resurrection of the Son as One who was now to be the life of the world.

But in the second place, the life-giving force that flowed from the Son's Sacrifice showed itself at the first Pentecost, in the vitalizing, recreating power the disciples knew as the Holy Spirit through whom the love of Father and Son is ceaselessly made available to the Church.

In the events of the first Christian Passover, from Calvary to the Cenacle, from Good Friday to Whitsun, we get the only exhibition of God's inner life that history affords: those events *are* that inner life projected into the public space of the human world.

So there's nothing accidental about the way we celebrate Trinity Sunday as soon as we've commemorated the events of Easter and Pentecost. Seen as the revelation of God as Trinity, those events which founded our religion give us our most basic understanding of what the Ground of reality is like. It is self-communicating, self-giving divine Love. They also give us the key to what our own lives should be like (God help us!). They should be the finite image of that love. And lastly they form the basis of our hope for the ultimate future of the world, when our flawed attempts to be the image of God can be mended and made whole in the context of the homecoming of all creation to its Goal, to its Source.

Thursday after Trinity Sunday, Solemnity of Corpus Christi (1)

The greatest act of our Creator was when, in the Incarnation, he made himself one of his own creatures so that we might be reconciled with him. And the greatest act of the incarnate Lord was his giving himself to his disciples as the Blessed Sacrament, so that his Incarnation and thus his reconciliation of the human race with the Father by his Death and Resurrection might be accessible in a sign which speaks to all human beings in a simple language, the language of nourishment and delight.

How extraordinary that the infinite God, the foundation of all existence and all thought, should have entered his own creation as one of his own creatures, so that grace might be poured out on us from within our human experience and we be brought to share his superabundant life of glory! None of the ancient philosophers ever grasped this truth: God is so divinely free in relation to the world that, without surrendering his infinite difference from it, he could enter the world as a finite being to become its true centre from within.

And how much in the style of this same God it is that, as the incarnate Word Jesus Christ, he should have made the saving climax of involvement with us his life-giving Death and Resurrection which sum up all he was and did and spoke as man: endlessly available through this Eucharistic sacrament, instituted on the night he was betrayed. In this sacrament he would continue to give himself, to pour himself out, as the celebrant pours wine into the chalice, and to distribute himself as the Host is distributed to countless disciples. We can tell that the Eucharistic Lord is the same as the Creator Lord because in this sacrament we see the hallmark of God as Christ revealed him to be. Self-giving is his *métier*.

The feast in whose radiant shadow we meet today, Corpus Christi, would not have been possible without a woman or, to be more precise, without two women. *Ave verum corpus*, we sing in the well-known Eucharistic antiphon, *natum ex Maria virgine*. 'Hail true Body, born of Mary the Virgin'. Without our Lady, no Christ, and so no Christianity. 'Give your answer quickly, Lady', wrote St Bernard, apostrophizing Mary of Nazareth in the moment of the Annunciation, 'for the salvation of the whole world turns on your response'. But if Mary is the Mother of the Church, we owe today's feast more specifically to one daughter of the Church, Juliana of Liège, a laywoman of holy life in thirteenth century Flanders, in the duchy of Burgundy, then the crossroads of the mediaeval West to which England also belonged.

Juliana's contribution is typical of the initiatives taken by women in the spiritual life of the Catholic Church, as they renewed in their own persons that deeper receptivity to the Word to which Mary had given perfect expression. Juliana took for granted the common symbolism, found in the Fathers as well as the mediaevals, whereby the Church was the moon reflecting light to the earth from the sun, Jesus Christ. But she saw that moon as partially eclipsed because the minds and hearts of the faithful were not focussed on what the Eucharistic sacrament involves. True, each Holy Week, on Maundy Thursday, they recalled its institution, but always against the background of our Lord's imminent Betrayal and Death. At the Eucharist of Holy Thursday, as at the original Last Supper, as described by the Gospel according to St John, it is always night. The night of human sin, of human malice, of human infidelity, englobed it. What was needed was a different sort of Thursday, a Thursday to celebrate in the light—in the happiness and joy of the Easter outcome of Christ's atoning work.

It would be, then as, triumphantly, it is a feast to give thanks for this sacrament as the abiding presence in the Church of the victorious Lamb. This is the Lamb who in his Resurrection has conquered not only sin but death and the divisive effects of time and now draws men and women to himself along all history's ways, all the roads of the earth.

Thursday after Trinity Sunday, Solemnity of Corpus Christi (2)

On his way to take Communion to some of the faithful in prison, a young deacon was waylaid by a mob. The condition for getting away in one piece was simple: hand over that little box round your neck. The box was a pyx. It contained particles of the Host consecrated that morning at the pope's Mass. The deacon preferred an alternative to handing over the Body of the Lord to mockery at pagan hands. He was beaten to death and his name, Tarcisius, is enrolled among the martyrs.

It's a story from third century Rome but no doubt there are places the world where it could happen today. Its interest lies in the way it brings out something of great importance about the Eucharist. The consecrated bread and wine are not just sacred symbols. The consecrated Eucharist is not on the same level as holy water or a crucifix or a picture of the Virgin. It is not on the same level as the materials of other signs that, like itself, are sacraments, instituted by the Saviour: the water of Baptism, or the oils used in confirming, ordaining, the anointing of the sick. It is in a different ball-game. It is not just a sacrament, it is the *Blessed* Sacrament.

The reason is straightforward. The other sacraments are gifts of God. This sacrament is a gift which contains the Giver. The other sacraments are signs of the action of Christ: Christ healing, Christ forgiving, or whatever. This sacrament, by contrast, is the sign of his sheer Presence among his own. So long as the outward forms of bread and wine endure, there he is, just willing and choosing to be there, to be present, to be for us.

And this plain difference tells us something profound about this sacrament. In spiritual books the Blessed Sacrament is said to be the sacrament of, in particular, God's *love*. That is not pious gush. It is characteristic of the behaviour of those who love that they wish to be present with each other just for the sake of it, just for the sake of being with them. Often enough the practical arrangements lovers make are hardly more than excuses for seeing more of each other. This is the way the Blessed Sacrament works. Christ on the altar, Christ in the tabernacle, Christ in the monstrance: here not to be useful but to be present, present for the simple delight of it.

Thursday after Trinity Sunday, Solemnity of Corpus Christi (3)

Today is one of those very *Catholic* days. The carrying of the consecrated Host in procession is a very Catholic thing to do, because that emphasis on the thereness—the hereness—of the Eucharistic Lord in all his glorious objectivity, accompanying his people on their pilgrimage through life, is a very Catholic emphasis. And we are glad for this. We rejoice in those emphases that give the Christian faith greater fullness, allow it to expand to the dimensions the divine generosity wants it to have. As someone said, I didn't become a Catholic to become a Protestant.

But of course the sacrament of unity was never meant to be something divisive in Christendom. The contrary is the case. We have only to think how modern-day historians of the Middle Ages, with their sociological bent, write of the functioning of this feast day in pre-Reformation England. They speak of Corpus Christi as the date of a yearly 'social miracle' whereby people put aside those more sectorial interests and concerns which were theirs as representatives of this or that group or class in a diversified society. Instead, on this day people found themselves united in the procession which centred so dramatically on their common Lord, present in his Eucharistic Body, a Body whose power to create unity held out to the social body in its everyday disunity the image they were to emulate, and if possible to realize.

Today an average Catholic congregation in this country is also diversified by variations in its interests and concerns, its attitude to public policy and cultural style, the generation gaps between its members, and so on. So we too must allow the same social miracle — the same cultural miracle — to happen for us, the same unity to flow from the Eucharistic Body to the fragmented social body.

Corpus Christi is a day of public corporate witness, either in city streets or through the fields, in the realm of nature, where man and beast are engaged together. But by exhibiting the Host for our personal contemplation, it is also a reminder that to rely simply and solely on the corporate experience of the Liturgy, vital as it is, is not wise. In the Christian life we are not to be loners, but nor are we simply to be carried along. We have to make a personal appropriation of what was done for us.

I have to be able to say 'My Jesus', and an excellent way in which to say those words is by looking with loving devotion toward the Host: the Host at the Mass, the Host at Benediction, the Host in the Eucharistic tabernacle. When we grasp to the extent we can what the God who came as man to the altar of sacrifice, the altar of the Cross, has done for us, we find it is easy (this is the message of the great adorers like Charles de Foucauld), to let ourselves be clothed in charity, thanks to the way our hearts and minds are moved.

Thursday after Trinity Sunday, Solemnity of Corpus Christi (4)

'This is my Body: take it' these words of the Saviour reported by St Paul give us today, Corpus Christi, quite literally our marching orders. Today we don't just give thanks in a sedentary fashion for the institution of the Eucharist, this sacrament which is so many things to us at once: our Lord's real Presence; the re-actualising of his Sacrifice on Calvary; the anticipation of heavenly feasting with all the saints in his Kingdom, and the means of my own deepest union with the other members of his Mystical Body, the Church, in Christ our common Head. Today something more is asked of us than at Mass on other days. We are required to be more mobile.

And this has to do with the active manifestation of the sacramental Lord to the world for which his saving Sacrifice was made.

Like so much in the devotional life of the Church, the feast of Corpus Christi originates in graces of mystical understanding given to women. In this case it was Juliana of Liège, in graces which enabled her to reach what the Church recognized to be an authentic insight into Tradition. Along the way of mystical understanding, the Holy Spirit taught Juliana that the reflection of the glory of the Eucharistic Lord was obscured in the Church by the lack of a festival of roughly this kind. In the symbolism she used, the moon of the Church was failing to reflect the light falling from its sun.

If we change the metaphor from visual to aural, we can say that what it was about was the need for fuller reverberations of the stupendous event of our salvation. In that event the Father, by raising Christ from the dead, brought all creation into union with his own immortal life, thanks to the now transfigured body of his dear Son. Christ has chosen in advance a sign to mark his loving Sacrifice broken bread, outpoured wine. These elements, once hallowed by their consecration in his name, are the first-fruits of a redeemed cosmos transparent to his glory until the time when the Son comes again at the end of time to begin his visible reign.

Where then can we hear the reverberations of all this in the devotional act distinctive to Corpus Christi, the Eucharistic procession? First, the reverberations are or should be sounding in us. In the procession, as we walk along, we should discover how the Lord is walking with his Church through the journey of life, whether that journey be for us confident or stumbling, until the end of time.

But then secondly the reverberations are in the environment; they are in the world around us. In the processional Host, the Saviour greets the city or the village, the street or the fields, the forest and the hedgerow, and all their denizens whether man or beast. Whichever they are, whoever they are, he is in the process of remaking their world, remaking it in that city of the New Jerusalem, described in the last book of the Bible, which is also a New Paradise with a river of life whose leaves will be for the healing of the nations and where also, so hints in Tradition assure us, the beasts too will have their place in a creation that is all restored.

Friday after the Second Sunday after Pentecost, Solemnity of the Sacred Heart

Just before the present Roman Calendar was introduced, in 1969, I remember attending Mass on the feast of the Sacred Heart which, it was rumoured, liturgists were seeking to abolish or at any rate demote. The preacher expressed satisfaction that this sentimental celebration which didn't even have the virtue of antiquity to recommend it, would soon be disappearing off our radar-screens. Shortly after, the new Calendar was published and the feast upgraded to a Solemnity. Actually, the rumours were not false, only incomplete. Later it became known that it was the pope, Paul VI, who had intervened personally to prevent the feast's demise.

What was the problem? I think a good deal of the difficulty came from nineteenth century art. For centuries, the only symbol of the Sacred Heart had been the crucifix, especially the kind which showed the five wounds, including the opened side of the Saviour with the bloody flux of water streaming out. Later, when artists began to depict the heart itself the effect was not always so happy, especially in the era of 'kitsch'.

The older imagery, by the way, shows how the feast had deep roots in Tradition. It is true that in the early modern period its emergence was hastened by the discovery of the crucial role of the heart in the circulation of blood, which gave the French spiritual theologian Jean Eudes the idea of recasting the whole of spirituality around the symbol of the heart, and he in his turn influenced St Margaret Mary Alacoque from whose encounters with Christ, seen as the Sacred Heart, the feast as we know it developed. But in itself the symbolism of the heart goes back through the Middle Ages to the Fathers and through them to the New Testament itself.

When we dig down to the bedrock of Scripture, which is always the foundation for true mysticism in the Church, we find that talk of hearts is far from sentimental. In the Bible, sheer feeling is represented by the bowels or 'innards', while the heart stands for understanding married with feeling, the intellectual and the affective rolled into one. The heart in Scripture is where one makes plans, the kind of plans that commit the whole of one's being. In this perspective, the piercing of the heart of Jesus on the Cross refers to the complete or total character of his Sacrifice for us. In taking upon himself the sin of the world, he could no longer plan and work for man's reconciliation with God but had simply to offer everything in trustful obedience to the Father, all earthly supports abandoned as he entered the darkness of death.

The sacrifice involved here is unimaginable without love. The heart thus becomes the symbol of Jesus' love for the Father, and, for the Father's sake, of his love for us as well. And not just the symbol! Strong affective reactions register as cardiac reflexes. The notion of dying of a broken heart is not *that* medically unsound.

The mystics of the Church understood this instinctively or, as we say, 'connaturally', by a second nature that comes from grace working on our first nature, the one we're born with. Thus St Catherine of Siena asks in her *Dialogue*:

> Sweet and spotless Lamb, you were dead when your side was opened: why did you want your heart to be thus wounded and opened? And she hears the Lord reply: My desire for the human race was endless but the actual act of the suffering and torments was finite. By that suffering I couldn't, then, demonstrate to you how much I loved you because my love was infinite. That's why I wanted to reveal to you the secret of my heart, by letting you see it open, so that you would understand how much it loved you, far more than I could have proved by a limited suffering.

Celebration of the Sacred Heart comes, then, from a fruitful collaboration between theologians and mystics. Between them, they brought to the surface a truth which is implicit in Scripture and, therefore, in the deposit of faith. It represents a deepening of the doctrine of the Incarnation. Today's Solemnity is in fact another Christmas. Not Christmas for children, responding to a baby's arrival. Christmas for adults who can relate to a grown man.

The Dedication of the Cathedral Church

Today is one of the few occasions in the Liturgy when we turn to look at the Church in and for herself. Normally, the Church is not an object of celebration in her own right. She is the medium by which we look at the object of our faith, or the context in which we do the looking. But today we perform an act of reflexion, a word whose basic meaning is to look in a mirror. We look at the mirror that shows us the divine life, and not by means of that mirror at the divine life itself.

Drawing on Scripture and Tradition, the Liturgy gives us a variety of images for the Church, the Body of Christ, the Bride of Christ, the Temple of the Spirit, the First-fruits of the Kingdom, all of which help to make this act of reflexion possible.

More specifically, though, on this day the Liturgy celebrates the mystery of the Church by celebrating its embodiment in one place: in the cathedral church of our diocese. This tells us something of importance. The mystery of the Church is found concretely in, with, and through a visible society: indeed, by way of an institution. The one can no more be separated from the other than the humanity of Christ can be separated from his divinity or his divinity from his humanity. The Church has two modes of being one mysteric and the other social or institutional, and it is not possible to prize them apart.

Nowadays, many people have a mainly sociological approach for which this Catholic concept of the Church is a difficulty. When this happens, we know that something has gone wrong with the ecclesial imagination, just as when people concentrate on the humanity of Christ at the expense of his divinity, we can tell that something has gone wrong with the Christological imagination.

If this happens, something will have gone wrong—most fundamentally—with our basic responsiveness to revelation. In the Church, our way of knowing is always sacramental: we always find the infinite in the finite, the invisible in the visible. The One who is infinite and invisible has made himself and his work finite and visible for the sake of our redemption. So today's feast invites us to reinvigorate our Christian imagination, and to lift up our hearts.

Coda: The Blessed Virgin Mary de Sabbato

At this Mass we are celebrating the memorial of the Blessed Virgin Mary 'on Saturday', or, in a more literal and, I think, thought-provoking translation, 'On the Sabbath'.

It's interesting, I find, that this is the only way the Church (or at least the Latin church) now marks when we do so mark it the Jewish Sabbath. Through the person of Mary we keep up a link with the sacred day of the Jews, and that is appropriate for Mary was a Jewess, and it was through her that the Word of God became not only a human being but a human being of the seed of Abraham, and so entered on the human patrimony prepared for him by his heavenly Father through so many centuries.

We can think today of the Jewish roots of our faith and enjoy a little of that natural peace and repose, that exemption from work and strain, that reliving of the happiness of the original creation which the Sabbath was and is.

But because we are not only spiritual Semites but also Christians, we can't stop there. The Sabbath with which Mary is forever associated is one particular Sabbath, a dark and terrible Sabbath, a Sabbath of silence, when on Holy Saturday Israel's Messiah slept the sleep of death.

Was that death, which we proclaim in every Mass, accompanied by no faith at all, no hope at all, from the side of his own people? Was there not, as the prophets had expected, at any rate a loyal remnant to give testimony to him? There was, and its name was Mary.

The classic art of the Church never portrays our Lady as it does Mary Magdalene, desperate and dishevelled at the entombment of Christ. The Mother is bowed but unbroken. Every Jewish mother on Sabbath lights the candles for the family. Just so, in her faith and hope, Mary kept the candles of the Sabbath alight for her Son. That is what we too are called to do by our faithfulness to Christ and the Church in a difficult time.

The garden of the old creation, like our own lives, has to pass by this way. The garden has been invaded by disorder. It is full of stinging nettles and the tangled roots of ground elder. Much of the grass has turned to moss and weeds. We can't expect to escape suffering and trials where even the Mother of God did not. But through Mary's faith and hope the covenant of God with Israel kept going on its human side when, in the death of the Redeemer it was under threat. Her faith and hope brought us through, into the new garden of the world of the Resurrection with its unalloyed joy that will never end.

Lightning Source UK Ltd.
Milton Keynes UK
UKOW042214021112

201610UK00001B/11/P